国家级一流本科课程配套教材

新思维英语写作

主　编　廖　敏

编　者　田　径　吕　汀　王凯凤

English Writing on Three Dimensions

清華大學出版社
北京

内容简介

本教材从学生实际需求出发，以有效输出为目标，涵盖写作热点话题，旨在全面提升学生的英语写作能力。本教材共分为两大部分。第一部分的八个单元为有效表达原则，系统搭建遣词造句、展句成段、修辞技巧与逻辑思辨等写作技能框架。第二部分包含八大实用写作话题：学习动机、社会关系、人类本性、性别问题、名人故事、商务世界、科技发展和环境保护。本教材内容新颖、体系完备、讲练结合、配套 MOOC，形成了英语写作"理论框架—话题储备—运用实操"的有机整体，以科学独特的新思维融会贯通英语写作各个维度，让读者一书在手、写作无忧。本教材另配有练习答案和 PPT 教学课件，读者可登录"清华社英语在线"（www.tsinghuaelt.com）进行下载。

本教材可作为大学英语写作教材，也适用于各高校结合相关课程展开混合式翻转教学；同时还可作为广大英语爱好者自主学习的写作参考书。

图书在版编目（CIP）数据

新思维英语写作 / 廖敏主编. —北京：清华大学出版社，2024.3
ISBN 978-7-302-63691-5

Ⅰ.①新…　Ⅱ.①廖…　Ⅲ.①英语–写作–高等学校–教材　Ⅳ.①H319.36

中国国家版本馆 CIP 数据核字（2023）第 100028 号

责任编辑：倪雅莉
封面设计：李伯骥
责任校对：王凤芝
责任印制：沈　露

出版发行：清华大学出版社
　　　　网　　址：https://www.tup.com.cn，https://www.wqxuetang.com
　　　　地　　址：北京清华大学学研大厦 A 座　　　邮　　编：100084
　　　　社 总 机：010-83470000　　　　　　　　　邮　　购：010-62786544
　　　　投稿与读者服务：010-62776969，c-service@tup.tsinghua.edu.cn
　　　　质 量 反 馈：010-62772015，zhiliang@tup.tsinghua.edu.cn
印 装 者：三河市龙大印装有限公司
经　　销：全国新华书店
开　　本：185mm×260mm　　**印　　张**：14.25　　**字　　数**：301 千字
版　　次：2024 年 3 月第 1 版　　　　　　　　**印　　次**：2024 年 3 月第 1 次印刷
定　　价：65.00 元

产品编号：091971-01

前 言

新时代对英语人才提出了新要求，面对全球化所带来的挑战与机遇，未来的英语类人才不仅需要具备扎实的语言基本功，更需要较强的逻辑思辨能力与过硬的英语书面表达能力。外语界早已就培养英语学习者批判性思维能力的重要性达成共识，然而行之有效的途径却一直求而未得。从语言、修辞与逻辑三大维度设计的MOOC"英语有效表达：语言、修辞与逻辑"直接对标批判性思维能力的提升，打造批判性思维立体框架和实用的有效表达工具。该课程于2017年在中国大学慕课平台上线，目前已开课十一轮，选课人数超过十万人次。课程以其科学的内容体系、新颖的设计视角，于2019年获国家精品在线开放课程认证，2020年入选首批国家级线上一流本科课程。

经过多轮的线上线下教学实践，课程团队不断改进课程内容体系，通过科学梳理英语写作表达体系，提炼批判性思维模式，基本完成了知识体系和能力体系的线上架构并打通从读到写的线下系统。基于这样的背景，我们萌发了编写这部线下课堂配套教材的想法，利用多模态的新媒体形式，提供丰富多元的学习资源，提升学生国际视野与中国情怀，帮助他们成长为肩负未来国家发展重任的新型人才。

◆ 教材特点

内容新颖、编排科学：与传统写作教材围绕写作技能进行内容编排的方式不同，本教材力求构建系统的写作表达体系，辅以话题输入，贯通英语写作，帮助广大英语学习者夯实英语语言基础，领略英语修辞魅力，培养批判性思维，练就过硬写作本领。

线上线下、体系完备：教材各个板块相对独立、自成体系，又相互补充、有机统一，既适合学生在学校老师的带领下混合翻转、系统学习、层层进阶，又适合广大英语爱好者自主泛在、碎片化的学习，构建线上线下的循环学习共同体。

对标考试、全面提升：本教材的写作练习设计有助于学生在知识、能力和话题储备的基础上形成新思维写作能力，提升写作应试能力。

❖ 教材内容

本教材分为两大部分。第一部分为有效表达原则，共八个单元，完全对应相关 MOOC 章节，构建从字词句段到篇章修辞与逻辑思辨的英语写作知识与能力体系；配套 MOOC 视频资源，真正做到多模态融会贯通。第二部分则为有效表达话题，涵盖八大实用写作话题：学习动机、社会关系、人类本性、性别问题、名人故事、商务世界、科技发展和环境保护。每个话题设 A 和 B 两篇文章，促使学生从不同方面看待问题，培养批判性思维习惯与能力。编者对 A 课文从语言、修辞和逻辑三个维度进行分析讲解，将本教材提倡的有效表达原则加以运用演示，同时对标英语考试写作题型与能力要求设计互动写作环节，促使学生对课文内容进行归纳提取，并针对其中的核心观点给出自己的见解。B 课文从语言、修辞和逻辑三个维度设计练习，引导学生学以致用，强化本教材提炼的写作原则并专设批判性思维写作习题，提升写作应试能力。本教材旨在通过全方位输入英语写作原则与话题，让学生具备新思维写作输出能力。

❖ 教材使用建议

使用方法一：

一、按照本教材顺序，先讲上篇英语有效表达原则八个章节（直接配合 MOOC 先后顺序）。教学时间安排：八周。

二、再讲下篇英语有效表达话题八个章节，将上篇所讲原则通过文章分析和练习加以运用。教学时间安排：八周。

特点： 先通过学习形成英语有效表达整体概念，然后在具体的文章中加以运用实践。通过学以致用，系统掌握有效表达原则，以全新思维提升学生英语写作能力。教师可利用高校课程展开混合式翻转教学；本教材也可以成为广大英语学习者自主泛在的学习资料。

使用方法二：

一、直接进入下篇英语有效表达话题八个章节，按话题安排教学进度。

二、在下篇章节的文章分析及练习部分涉及上篇的表达原则时，根据提示链接到上篇相关内容及 MOOC 进行学习。

三、建议两周一个话题，总共十六周。

特点：直接从话题入手，容易引起学生的兴趣。在学习中遇到具体的写作现象实例时，再链接相关表达原则加以分析解释，更利于接受。从现象到本质的学习方式也更为自然。社会学习者也完全可以轻松驾驭。

❖ 编者团队

本教材编写团队中三名教师为建设配套 MOOC 的原班人马，新增一名博士，均有 15 年以上的高校英语教学经验。具体编写任务分工如下：廖敏负责全书的框架体例设计与统稿校对；第一、第二单元由吕汀编写；第三、第四单元由田径编写；第五、第六单元由王凯凤编写，吴冰提供 MOOC 底稿；第七、第八单元由廖敏编写。特别感谢电子科技大学规划教材项目（项目代码：Y030202062003001054）提供初期经费支持。衷心感谢电子科技大学外国语学院对本教材编写的大力支持。李皓婷、蒋析彤、王岚、陈治州、刘子睿等研究生参与了资料收集、整理校对等，在此深表谢意。教材内容大都来自多年的真实课堂实践，有些案例及教学内容参阅相关图书、课程、讲座、网页等资源，在此一并表示由衷感谢与真诚敬意。在参考文献中我们尽量罗列出资料来源，但因日积月累，且内容广泛，难免挂一漏万，再加上精力有限，教材中难免存在一些错漏，还望学界前辈、专家同仁及教材使用者不吝赐教，以便我们不断改进，进一步提高教材质量。

编者

2023 年 9 月

Contents

Part I Rules for Effective Expression

Part II Topics for Effective Expression

Unit 2   Social Connection 115

    Text A   Weak-Tie Friendships May Mean More than You Think 115

        Effective Expression: A Linguistic Dimension 118

        Effective Expression: A Rhetorical Dimension 119

        Effective Expression: A Logical Dimension 119

        Interactive Writing 120

    Text B   "Sorry, I Was Distracted…" 121

        Effective Expression in Practice 123

        Critical Thinking in Practice 125

Unit 3   Human Traits 126

    Text A   The Power of Grit 126

        Effective Expression: A Linguistic Dimension 129

        Effective Expression: A Rhetorical Dimension 131

        Effective Expression: A Logical Dimension 132

        Interactive Writing 133

    Text B   Angela Duckworth Responds to a New Critique of Grit 134

        Effective Expression in Practice 137

        Critical Thinking in Practice 139

Unit 4   Gender Issues 140

    Text A   Man, Weeping 140

        Effective Expression: A Linguistic Dimension 143

        Effective Expression: A Rhetorical Dimension 145

        Effective Expression: A Logical Dimension 147

        Interactive Writing 148

    Text B   Born to Be Different? 149

        Effective Expression in Practice 152

        Critical Thinking in Practice 154

Unit 5   Celebrities 155

    Text A   The Woman Behind the Wizard 155

        Effective Expression: A Linguistic Dimension 158

        Effective Expression: A Rhetorical Dimension 163

        Effective Expression: A Logical Dimension 165

        Interactive Writing 166

    Text B   Ode to Beethoven 167

        Effective Expression in Practice 170

        Critical Thinking in Practice 173

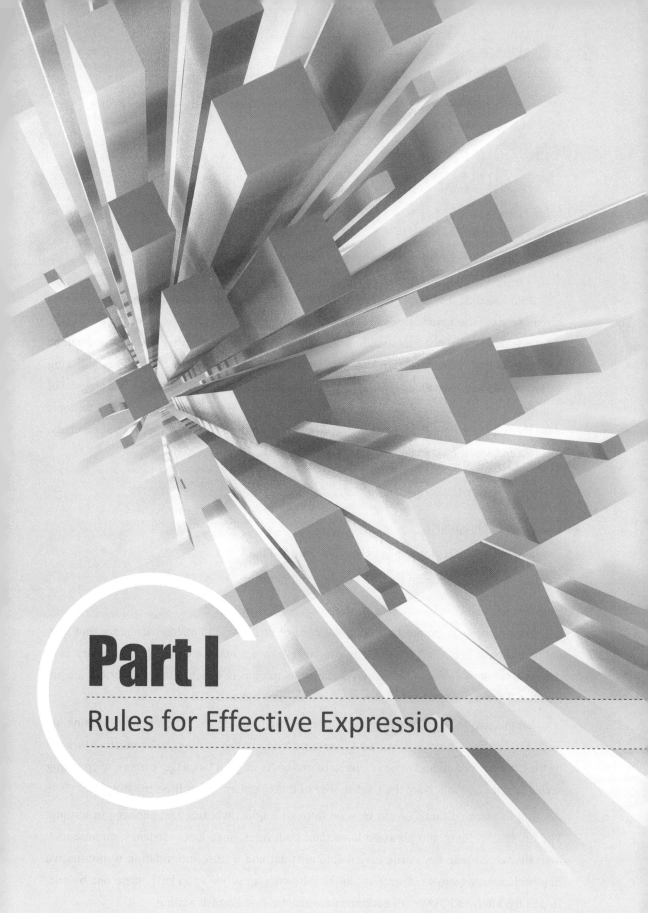

Part I

Rules for Effective Expression

Unit 1
Wording and Phrasing (I)

Both wording and phrasing involve the choice of words and the language style in a given context. The gerunds of the words and phrases mainly mean how to use words and phrases instead of simply understanding and remembering them. Wording and phrasing can be decomposed into choosing the right words, using varied sentence structures and establishing the appropriate tone. Apparently, without a good command of wording and phrasing, the progress of English learning will be hindered. Therefore, two units are set at the beginning to explore the topic about them. In this unit, the significance of learning wording and phrasing, lexical diversity, concrete and specific language and signal words are discussed.

Significance of Learning Wording and Phrasing

Lead-in Questions:

1. What is the relationship between language and thinking?

2. Why should we learn English wording and phrasing?

Vocabulary may be the first thing we need to write well in another language, but may not be the most important one. This is similar to how we make a building. Vocabulary is to writing what bricks are to a building. What matters more is in which fashion the bricks are put together. Therefore, we need to know the "fashion" in English writing.

Language is the carrier of thinking. Different languages denote different ways of thinking, so do English and Chinese. When we Chinese write in English, we tend to be much influenced by the Chinese way of thinking, even unconsciously. As English language learners, overcoming such influence and following the English way of thinking may be our life-time struggle.

English way of thinking can be seen through English wording and phrasing in writing. The English wording and phrasing have their own rules, such as consistency, conciseness, diversity, etc. These keywords may sound abstract and a little intimidating to non-native English language learners. Therefore, in the following units, we will clarify them one by one. Hopefully, afterwards, you will get some new insights into English writing.

1.2 Lexical Diversity

Lead-in Questions:

1. What is lexical diversity?

2. How can we achieve lexical diversity?

Scan the paragraph below and find out all the expressions that mean unhappy.

e.g.1. I enjoy all kinds and styles of music and how I feel at the moment can determine what music I may listen to. When I am happy and in a great mood then I like to listen to good old rock and roll or the blues. When I am more in a quiet mood or a little under the weather then some alternative rock, classical or maybe jazz suits my listening pleasure and when I am down in the dumps I prefer classical music to help calm the nerves. When, however, I really get depressed there is only one piece of music that helps to pull me out of that depression. When I am down, I turn to Ludwig Van Beethoven and his Ninth Symphony also known as *Ode to Joy*. It is, as far as I am concerned, the greatest piece of music ever written.

In this paragraph, "under the weather" "down in the dumps" "get depressed" and "down" all mean unhappy. Lexical diversity refers to the degree of employing different expressions for the same idea. It is a very important index of your command of English. In some international English tests, such as TOEFL and IELTS, lexical diversity has been used as an important index to grade the writings of the test-takers.

Let's check another paragraph for different expressions about time.

e.g.2. It was the best of times, it was the worst of times; it was the age of wisdom, it was the age of foolishness; it was the epoch of belief, it was the epoch of incredulity; it was the season of Light, it was the season of Darkness; it was the spring of hope, it was the winter of despair.

(Charles Dickens, *A Tale of Two Cities*, p.1)

Even in such a short paragraph, Dickens employed four different words to mean time: "times" "age" "epoch" and "season". This is lexical diversity, one of the symbols of good writing. Lexical diversity is opposite to repetition, which adds some color and dynamic change to the language. Color and dynamic change will increase the readability of the writing, thus attracting more readers. Lexical diversity will make the writing more appealing.

Since lexical diversity is important and useful, what should we do to improve it?

We should be aware of this issue. Being more careful and sensitive to different expressions of the same idea will help us to accumulate the expressions. It is always a headache for us to remember new words. But if we put words and expressions in groups, we will feel much easier. Take "bad mood" as an example. When we group the expressions like "under the weather" "down in the dumps" "down" "in low spirit" "in bad mood" together, instead of remembering them separately, we may feel it easier to remember them because of the semantic connection between them. While accumulating some expressions about bad mood, we may ask ourselves what expressions mean good mood. Then we will build up a new group of expressions about good mood, such as "overjoyed" "content" "pleased" "over the moon", etc.

The first step is to enlarge vocabulary. Interestingly, to enlarge the vocabulary, lexical diversity will also help. They form a two-way interactive relationship.

Now, let's have a look at several sentences you may be very familiar with.

e.g.3. We must <u>do our best</u> to <u>protect</u> buildings of historical interest.

e.g.4. It is <u>clear</u> that violent movies <u>are bad to</u> the lives of lots of kids.

e.g.5. <u>Nowadays</u>, human beings <u>face</u> big challenges in many areas.

All the underlined expressions are favored by Chinese English learners. Maybe we can try to replace them with some other expressions. For the first sentence, replace "do our best" with "do our utmost", and replace "protect" with "preserve". For the second sentence, "clear" can be replaced by "apparent", and "are bad to" can be replaced by "are harmful to". And for the last sentence, we may say "currently" or "at present time" for "nowadays", and we may use "are confronted with" for "face".

The second step is to consciously use different expressions in familiar contexts. We tend to use the most familiar expressions, because we feel safe this way. But sometimes, we need to jump out of the comfort zone to make change and make progress. Actually, sticking to the most familiar words is called fossilization of language in linguistics, and it will definitely hinder the progress of language learning.

 Concrete and Specific Language

Lead-in Questions:

1. What is concrete and specific language?

2. How can we use concrete and specific language?

Sometimes, we just take the two words, "concrete" and "specific", as the same thing. But there are some subtle differences between them. It's important to understand abstract and concrete language and general and specific language.

Abstract words refer to intangible qualities, ideas, and concepts. These words indicate things we know only through our intellect, like "truth" "honor" "kindness" and "grace". By comparison, concrete words refer to tangible qualities or characteristics, things we know through our senses. Words and phrases like "102 degrees" and "obese cat" are concrete.

An example may help us to get a clearer idea.

e.g.6. To excel in college, you'll have to work hard.

In this sentence, "work hard" is an abstract quality of a student. What behaviors can be regarded as "work hard" depends on the interpretation of readers. We may rephrase "work hard" into more concrete language.

e.g.7. To excel in college, you'll need to go to every class, do all your reading before you go, write several drafts of each paper and review your notes for each class weekly.

In this rephrased sentence, "work hard", this abstract idea, has been rephrased into a series of specific behaviors that can demonstrate the diligence of a student. In brief, we understand the abstract through our mental processes and interpret the concrete through our senses. There is some overlap between the two pairs of concepts. Now let's have a look at an example about general and specific.

Comparatively speaking, some words are more general or more specific in meaning rather than others. "Professionals", for instance, is more general than "scientists" "doctors" "teachers" "lawyers" "journalists", etc. But "scientists" may be regarded as a general word when compared with "chemists" or "physicists". Therefore, being general or specific is a relative concept. Relatively speaking, general words refer to larger classes or broader areas, and specific words refer to particular items or individual cases in smaller classes or narrower areas. Although both abstract and general words are useful, we are usually supposed to make efforts to master and use concrete and specific words wherever possible.

Now let's have a look at this list of words. Have you found out anything special about them?

e.g.8. food
      junk food
      dessert

ice cream

premium ice cream

Ben and Jerry's ice cream

Ben and Jerry's Chunky Monkey ice cream

a double-scoop waffle cone of Ben and Jerry's Chunky Monkey ice cream

They are more and more concrete and specific. We call this Ladder of Abstraction. Most words do not fall sharply into categories: They are not always abstract or concrete, general or specific. Moreover, the abstract and general often overlap, as do the concrete and specific. Therefore, it can be easier to classify words by placing them on a scale or continuum—a Ladder of Abstraction. The lower on the scale, the more concrete and specific the word is. On this scale, "ice cream" is more specific than "dessert", but more general than "premium ice cream".

Let's do some exercises. Take the general or abstract term down from three levels. First, have a look at the example:

e.g.9. junk food   dessert   ice cream   Chunky Monkey

The words become more and more concrete and specific. Now, do the same abstraction about the following two words.

students   _____   _____   _____
boring   _____   _____   _____

For "students", the answers can be "college students" "Chinese college students" and "Peking University students". And since "boring" is an abstract word, the following words should be more and more concrete. "Dull" "a dull play" and "a dull play about cooking and eating" can serve the same purpose.

Being specific and concrete can be informative and expressive. In order to be more specific and concrete, more relevant details need to be included, which will engage readers more.

Signal Words

Lead-in Questions:

1. What are signal words?

2. How can we understand signal words?

All passages have signposts to show the directions of the author's thoughts. But we use another expression, signal words. Have a look at the following example:

e.g.10. I love drinking tea. It keeps me awake at night.

What is the relationship between the two sentences? Why is the second sentence there? One explanation might be "It keeps me awake at night" is one of the reasons for loving drinking tea. Another explanation might be "Even though tea keeps me awake night, I still love drinking it". Both explanations make some sense, but we cannot be sure about either one. Why? Because there is no signal word. Without signal words, we may get lost in understanding the meaning. Just like without signposts, we don't know which way to go. If we add signal words in between, the meaning will be clearer. For example:

e.g.11. I love drinking tea, because it keeps me awake at night.

I love drinking tea, even though it keeps me awake at night.

Signal words are also called transitional words. They show the logical organization and improve the understandability, as well as connections and transitions between thoughts. Different relationships demand different signal words, and different signal words reflect different relationships. Now, let's have a look at some valuable types of signal words.

The first type is emphasis words, through which the author tells you directly that a particular idea or detail is especially important. Think of such words as red flags that the author is using to make sure you pay attention to a certain idea. Check the following paragraph:

e.g.12. Chronic air pollution is expensive to the American public, costing us dearly in terms of both money and health... It is especially in terms of health that pollution hurts. It is estimated that breathing the air of New York City is the equivalent of smoking two packs of cigarettes a day.

In this case, "especially" is the emphasis word and it directs the readers' attention to the health damage the pollution makes. The emphasis word immediately helps us get the idea the author wants to emphasize.

Here come the commonly-used emphasis words.

- important to note
- a primary concern
- the main value
- most noteworthy
- most of all
- a key feature
- especially valuable
- remember that

- a major event
- the principal item
- the chief factor
- above all
- especially relevant

- the chief outcome
- pay particular attention to
- a vital force
- a central issue
- the most substantial issue

Now, let's read another example:

e.g.13. A computer is often called a "thinking machine", and in many ways it is just that. Computers perform difficult and time-saving mathematical computations, as well as problems in logic and reasoning. In addition, computers run other machines and answer questions. Also, they are used to guide astronauts on takeoff.

"As well as" and "in addition" are the signal words here. This type of signal words is more like the green traffic light, indicating that the author's thought is going to continue in the same direction. This type of signal words is called addition words. They suggest that the author adds more detail or point of the same kind. Addition words are also used to list things. The following items are the commonly-used addition words.

- also
- finally
- first of all
- furthermore
- last of all
- moreover
- and
- the third reason

- another
- first
- for one thing
- in addition
- likewise
- next
- second

Besides the emphasis words and addition words, there are other types, such as "by contrast" "to illustrate this" and "thus". All these expressions are signal words, which can be categorized into three types. The first one is contrast. It signals a change in the direction of the author's thought. The author is pointing out a difference between two subjects or statements. The second one is illustration. With that, we know an example is going to be provided. As for the third one, there is a cause-and-effect relationship in between.

Now it's time to summarize what has been discussed in this topic. Signal words are like the glue that holds the ideas together. Thus, the writing becomes a unified piece. Five types of signal words have been introduced: emphasis words, addition words, contrast words, illustration words and cause-and-effect words. In reading, we should try to make use of the signal words to clarify the major thoughts of the author. In writing, we should also try to apply these signal words to make our own writings more coherent and logical.

Exercises

I. Mark true (T) or false (F) for the following statements.

1. Wording and phrasing are the same thing.   (   )
2. Lexical diversity refers to employing various words or phrases for the same idea. (   )
3. Lexical diversity is an important index of a good command of English.   (   )
4. Specific language and concrete language share some common traits, but not the same.   (   )
5. Any words or phrases can be categorized as either specific or non-specific.   (   )
6. Signal words can help clarify ideas.   (   )
7. Addition words are more like red traffic lights, suggesting the readers to stop.   (   )
8. Transitional words or phrases usually work as signal words.   (   )

II. Identify the signal words from the list below. Mark Y for the signal words and N for the non-signal words. If they are signal words, specify their specific types.

1. what's more	( )	5. on the contrary	( )
2. therefore	( )	6. according to	( )
3. to justify this	( )	7. in particular	( )
4. interesting	( )	8. first of all	( )

III. Use the words and phrases in the box to replace the underlined parts in each sentence.

(a) resonate	(b) vacation destinations	(c) a wide range of
(d) metropolitan	(e) is located	(f) affordable
(g) can get inspired with	(h) have free access to the	(i) with free entrance
(j) definitely		

_____ 1. This (1) <u>very big</u> Canadian city Toronto is just a 90-minute trip from 60 percent of the United States.

_____ 2. Providence is terrific for families, especially high school kids since the capital city is home to (2) <u>a lot of different</u> colleges (Brown University, Johnson & Wales, Rhode Island School of Design), where they (3) <u>want to learn more from</u> campus tours and on-campus museums.

_____ 3. Known for its natural beauty, sustainability, and outdoor activities, Portland is a favorite option for (4) <u>inexpensive</u> family vacations.

_____ 4. The Lake Cumberland State Resort Park (5) <u>lies</u> on one of the ten largest man-made lakes in the country, and it's one of the top (6) <u>places for travellers</u> in the eastern United States.

_____ 5. All the park lodging starts at around $100 per night, including DuPont Lodge, the Cottages, and Woodland Rooms, which (7) <u>include free</u> indoor pools, and also include free meals to kids 5 and under at the restaurant.

_____ 6. Martin Luther King Jr Birthplace and Memorial is a National Park (8) <u>free for visitors</u>; walking in the footsteps of history here will (9) <u>certainly</u> (10) <u>cause something to echo</u> with your kids.

IV. Use the words and phrases in the box to fill in the blanks.

(a) tree-lined streets	(b) rolling green hills	(c) skyscrapers dotting its skylines
(d) confluence	(e) the hub of the sprawling metropolitan region	
(f) compact downtown area	(g) tucked	(h) a number of historical landmarks
(i) concentration of restaurants and food stores		(j) babies and toddlers

1. Beaches are a great fit for _____ who can spend endless hours playing with you in the sand and surf.

2. This area of Boston contains _____, including the Old State House, Granary Burial Ground, and Old South Meeting House.

3. The heart of this modern city Boston is the _____, which serves as the city's commercial and financial district.

4. Take Exit 1 from New Jersey's Garden State Parkway and you'll discover this charming Victorian beach town with _____.

5. New York is a metropolitan with _____ .

6. On the southern end of the district is Chinatown, with its _____ .

7. Washington, D. C. is located at the _____ of the Potomac and Anacostia rivers.

8. The seat of King County, Seattle is _____ (of Greater Seattle) and is the largest city in Washington.

9. Bowling Green, located just an hour north of Nashville, is _____ in among the _____ of South Central Kentucky's Cave Country.

V. Match the signal words with their functions.

1. 附加	a. after, meanwhile, now, before, when, while
2. 列举	b. in summary, to sum up, in conclusion, in a word
3. 对比	c. and, furthermore, moreover, besides, in addition, too
4. 重复	d. first(ly), last (but not least), next, in the first place
5. 因果	e. though, although, even if, even though
6. 顺序	f. above all, extremely, completely, totally, indeed
7. 总结	g. for instance, for example, such as
8. 让步	h. but, however, on the contrary
9. 时间	i. in other words, namely, that is (to say)
10. 强调	j. since, because, so, thus, hence, therefore

Unit 2
Wording and Phrasing (II)

In this unit, we will continue to discuss wording and phrasing. Some subtopics will be covered including pronoun clarity, concise language, consistent language and syntactic variety. As mentioned in Unit 1, wording and phrasing are mainly about how to use words and phrases in given contexts. Without the proper use of words and phrases, an adequate command of English can never be achieved.

 Pronoun Clarity

Lead-in Questions:

1. Why should we use pronouns?

2. What is pronoun clarity?

3. How can we achieve pronoun clarity?

First of all, read the sentence below:

e.g. 1. For more details about our product, contact us on 12345678 or visit their website.

Apparently, the changing of pronoun from "our" "us" to "their" makes the readers confused. Who is the company and who is the outsider? This is inconsistency of pronouns.

Let's talk about what a pronoun is. "I" "we" "they" "she" "he", and so on are pronouns. Besides, a pronoun is a word that is used in place of a noun. "He" replaces "John", "her" replaces "Suzie's", and so on. And the word or phrase that the pronoun refers to and replaces is called its antecedent. Then, why should we use pronouns?

Let's check the following example:

e.g. 2. Jane enjoys playing the violin. Jane plays the violin every evening. Jane's brother becomes annoyed when Jane practices.

This text looks very awkward. Using pronouns will help simplify it.

e.g. 3. Jane enjoys playing the violin. She plays the violin every evening. Her brother becomes annoyed when she practices.

When the passage is revised by using pronouns, it conveys the same information but much more concisely. Besides, the passage becomes more like a unified one instead of being put together with several independent sentences.

A pronoun and its antecedent work closely together to make a sentence clear in meaning. There are some tips for getting such clarity.

Tip 1: Make a pronoun refer clearly to one antecedent.

For example:

e.g. 4. Hemingway is sometimes compared with Jack London, but he was quite different.

In Example 4, we may get confused about who "he" actually stands for, since either Hemingway or Jack London can work.

Take another example:

e.g. 5. Employees should consult with the supervisor who required personal time.

According to Example 5, we may think "who" refers to employees. But English is such a language that demands a high degree of clarity. We should make the sentence clearer by changing the place of who clause. In Example 6, the meaning is much clearer.

e.g. 6. Employees who required personal time should consult with the supervisor.

Tip 2: Place a pronoun close enough to its antecedent to ensure clarity.

For example:

e.g. 7. Vincent found a lamp in the attic that his aunt had used.

Here we don't know what his aunt had used, lamp or attic. It's really confusing. If we revise it into the following sentence, either one is clearer than the original sentence.

e.g. 8. Vincent found a lamp that his aunt had used in the attic. / In the attic that Vincent's aunt had used, he found a lamp.

Tip 3: Make a pronoun refer to a specific antecedent, not an implied one.

A pronoun should refer to a specific noun or other pronoun. But when such pronouns as "this" "that" "which" or "it" are used, the guessing of the implied reference may occur. Let's have a look at the following example:

e.g. 9. I can be kind to people, **which** is more than you can.

Here "which" refers to the whole preceding clause. Such reference is often called broad reference. But we should be very careful in using this reference. If the pronouns confuse readers, we should avoid using it and provide an appropriate noun. For example:

e.g. 10. The faculty agreed on changing the requirements, but **it** took time.

Here, the meaning of it is confusing. Does "it" mean this agreement or changing process? We don't know. In order to clarify it, we may revise the sentence as follows:

e.g. 11. The faculty agreed on changing the requirements, but the agreement took time. / The faculty agreed on changing the requirements, but the change took time.

Tip 4: Use "it" or "they" to refer to definite antecedents.

In conversations we commonly use expressions such as "It says in the paper" or "They say". But such indefinite use of "it" or "they" is inappropriate in writing. The constructions are not only unclear but wordy. For example:

e.g. 12. In this latest movie, it depicts the early settlement on the American continent.
e.g. 13. In the average TV series, they present a false picture of life.

Some students often confuse the writing with speaking in language choice. A sentence of this kind often appears in their writings. We can revise them as follows:

e.g. 14. This latest movie depicts the early settlement on the American continent.
e.g. 15. The average TV series present a false picture of life.

The revised sentences become not only clearer in meaning but also more concise in language.

2.2 Concise Language

Lead-in Questions:

1. Why should we pay attention to concise language?

2. How can we achieve conciseness?

"Less is more" is a golden rule in English writing. It means we should try to avoid using meaningless expressions and make every word count. This is what we will discuss here, being concise. Let's read the following sentences:

e.g. 16. The cover of the book is red in color.

e.g. 17. Professor Smith is a very learned and kind professor.

e.g. 18. In my opinion, I think the second plan is better.

They all sound kind of redundant. Some words can be deleted. In Example 16, "red" and "color" are repetitive. In Example 17, "professor" has been used twice, which is unnecessary. In Example 18, "in my opinion" and "I think" mean the same thing. One is enough. Therefore, the three sentences can be revised as follows:

e.g. 19. The book cover is red.

e.g. 20. Professor Smith is very learned and kind.

e.g. 21. I think the second plan is better.

Compared with the original three sentences, the three new ones are more concise.

Being concise means effective sentence should not contain extra or unnecessary words. Many students think that long sentences with many words will make their writing more impressive. But in fact, almost every reader values conciseness, since concise writing is usually easier to read, better thought out, and better organized—that is, simply better writing. Being concise and being brief are different. Concise usually means not just brief but packed with information. Then how to be concise? There are some practical tips.

Tip 1: Revise wordy sentence structures.

What are wordy sentence structures? Chinese students like to use "it be" or "there be" structures. Such structures can be rhetorically effective for emphasis in some situations, but overuse or unnecessary use of these structures creates wordiness. For example:

e.g. 22. There are thirteen courses offered by the Department of Languages.

e.g. 23. It is the governor who signs bills.

The two sentences can be revised into more concise versions:

e.g. 24. The Department of Languages offered thirteen courses.
e.g. 25. The governor signs bills.

The revised version contains the same amount of information but has fewer words, which makes the sentences more concise.

Tip 2: Change clauses to phrases, phrases to single words.

Now, have a look at this sentence:

e.g. 26. The Titanic which was a huge ocean liner sank in 1812.

Do you have any methods to make it more concise?

e.g. 27. The Titanic, a huge ocean liner, sank in 1812.

This is the second method to achieve conciseness. But some students are obsessed with long sentences. Writing long sentences is only a writing practice for students to improve language command. The length of sentences does not actually represent your writing competence. Instead, we should keep in mind that the form serves for the content. Now, let's see another example:

e.g. 28. The Channel Tunnel, which runs between Britain and France, bores through a bed of solid chalk that is twenty-three miles across.

The clause can be shortened to "between Britain and France". Now, let's see some more clauses.

- a car which was going south
- a person who is attractive
- his brother, who is a member

We can revise them as follows:

- a car going south
- an attractive person
- his brother, a member

Tip 3: Cut unnecessary repetition.

Let's have a look at the sentence below.

e.g. 29. President Kennedy was assassinated and killed.

"Assassinate" means to murder someone well-known, so "killed" is redundant. The third method is to cut unnecessary repetition. Let's see some other examples:

e.g. 30. Many unskilled workers without training in a particular job are unemployed and do not have any work.

In Example 30, "without training in a particular job" and "unskilled" share the same meaning and "do not have any work" actually means "unemployed". Therefore, we can revise the sentence as follows:

e.g. 31. Many unskilled workers are unemployed.

Besides, the use of one word in two different ways within a sentence is confusing. For example:

e.g. 32. Preschool instructors play a role in the child's understanding of male and female roles.

In Example 32, the repetition of "role" is confusing and thus unnecessary. We may use "part" to replace the first "role".

 Consistent Language

Lead-in Questions:

1. Why should we pay attention to consistent language?

2. How can we achieve consistency?

Let's see the following paragraph:

e.g. 33. A bank commonly owes more to its customers than is held in reserve. They kept enough assets to meet reasonable withdrawals, but panicked customers may demand all their deposits. Then demands will exceed supplies, and banks failed. These days, a person's losses are not likely to be great because the government insures your deposits.

This paragraph is not clear in meaning, because the inconsistencies in grammatical elements will distort the meaning and confuse readers. English, as an alphabetic language, has very strict grammatical rules to follow. How to keep consistency definitely needs our attention and efforts. Here are some tips.

Tip 1: Keep consistency in person and number.

Person in grammar refers to the distinction between the first person, the second person and the third person. Why do the shifts in person often occur? Because we can use either the second person or the third person to refer to people in general. For example:

e.g. 34. People should not drive after they drink alcohol. /

One should not drive after he or she drinks alcohol. /

You should not drive after you drink alcohol.

Any of the three sentences is acceptable in certain context. But a mixture of them is inconsistent and unacceptable. For example:

e.g. 35. People should not drive after you drink alcohol. /

One should not drive after they drink alcohol.

Now, let's see the following sentence:

e.g. 36. If a person works hard, you can accomplish a great deal.

Here, "a person" and "you" are not consistent. We can change either of them. For example:

e.g. 37. If a person works hard, he or she can accomplish a great deal. / If you work hard, you can accomplish a great deal.

Then, what's the consistency in number? Number refers to the distinction between singular and plural. Here come more examples:

e.g. 38. When taxpayers do not file their return early, they will not get a refund quickly.

Is anything wrong with the sentence? "Taxpayers" are in plural form. They should file their "returns" rather than "return", and get "refunds" rather than "a refund". This is inconsistency in number, which breaks the logical agreement between the nouns.

Tip 2: Keep consistency in tense and mood.

Different from Chinese, English has a strict tense system. All the verbs in a sentence should be consistent. Have a look at this sentence:

e.g. 39. Ramon will graduate from college thirty years after his father arrived in the United States.

This sentence is wrong, because "will graduate" and "arrived" are not consistent. Then we can revise it as follows:

e.g. 40. Ramon graduated from college thirty years after his father had arrived in the United States.

How to use tense right and keep tense consistent are always difficult for Chinese students, partly because Chinese does not have tenses. Being consistent not only applies to one sentence, but also to a paragraph, a passage. Besides, in the compound sentence, the tense of the clause should be consistent with the tense of the main sentence. That means, if the main sentence is in past tense, then the clause should be in past tense too. For example:

e.g. 41. He said he will come to our home tomorrow.

Here, "will" should be changed to "would" because of "said" in the main sentence. We should take the sentence as a whole. Do not just focus on one part of it.

The shifts in the mood of verbs occur most frequently in directions when the author moves between the imperative mood and the indicative mood. We may get a clearer picture in the following sentence:

e.g. 42. Cook the mixture slowly, and you should stir it until the sugar is dissolved.

"Cook the mixture slowly" is the imperative mood, but "you should stir it until the sugar is dissolved" is the indicative mood. Since imperative mood is clearer in giving instructions than indicative mood, we'd better change the indicative mood to the imperative mood. Then we can revise the sentence as follows:

e.g. 43. Cook the mixture slowly, and stir it until the sugar is dissolved.

Therefore, the mood here is not about the mood of the person. It is about the human mood but conveyed through language.

Tip 3: Keep consistency in subject and voice.

Now, it's time about the third consistency, being consistent in subject and voice. When a verb is in the active voice, the subject is the actor; when a verb is in the passive voice, the subject is the receiver of the action. A shift in voice may sometimes help focus the reader's attention on a single subject, as in Example 44:

e.g. 44. The candidate campaigned vigorously and was nominated on the first ballot.

The subject "candidate" has been emphasized in this way. But, most shifts in voice also involve shifts in subject. They are unnecessary and confusing. For example:

e.g. 45. If students learn how to study efficiently, much better grades will be made.

The voice is changed from active in the clause to passive in the main sentence. Thus, the subject of the clause also changes from "students" to "much better grades". Such shifts in voice and subject are not necessary. We can revise the sentence into a clearer version:

e.g. 46. If students learn how to study efficiently, they will get much better grades on tests.

Let's see two more examples:

e.g. 47. Conscientious students begin to prepare for tests immediately after the first class is attended.
e.g. 48. In class they listen carefully and good notes are taken.

Make the following two sentences consistent in subject and voice, and we may get two different sentences:

e.g. 49. Conscientious students begin to prepare for tests immediately after they attend the first class.
e.g. 50. In class they listen carefully and take good notes.

 Syntactic Variety

Lead-in Questions:

1. What is syntactic variety?

2. How can we achieve syntactic variety?

Lexical diversity refers to the degree of employing different expressions for the same idea. Here, we will move up our discussion on variety to a higher level, sentence level. In order to be distinguished from lexical diversity, syntactic variety is used here.

Syntactic variety is mainly about the relationship between sentences. In a paragraph or an essay, each sentence stands in relation to those before and after it. To make sentences work together effectively, we need to vary their length, structure, and word order to reflect the importance and complexity of ideas. Variety sometimes takes care of itself, but we can practice some established techniques for achieving syntactic variety. Before addressing some useful techniques for varying sentences, read the following paragraph:

> e.g. 51. A girl of 2 walked away from her parents. The girl was run over by a white van. The driver didn't stop to look at the girl. Then, the girl was struck by another vehicle. Several cars and people walked past the toddler.

This is a sad story, but the language cannot show the sadness, maybe because all the sentences are between eight and nine words long. They all begin with the subject, and they are equally detailed. This is an example demonstrating a lack of syntactic variety.

Then, we will discuss how to achieve it.

Tip 1: Vary sentence length and structure.

In most contemporary writing, sentences vary from 10 to 40 words, with an average of 15 to 25 words. If all the sentences are very long, the readers may get lost in details; and if all the sentences are very short, all the ideas seem equally important and the links between them may not be clear. Therefore, for long sentences, we can break them down, and for short sentences, we can combine them. Let's have a look at an example:

> e.g. 52. The moon is now drifting away from the earth. It moves away at the rate of about one inch a year. This movement is lengthening our days. They increase a thousandth of a second every year.

This is a string of brief and simple sentences. The logical connection between sentences is loosened by such a string. Then we may revise the four sentences as follows:

> e.g. 53. The moon is now drifting away from the earth about one inch a year. At a thousandth of a second every century, this movement is lengthening our days.

In the revised version, we can clearly see the logic connection between sentences. And the sentence length and structure also vary.

Tip 2: Vary sentence beginnings.

Varying sentence beginnings is also a useful way to diversify a sentence. An English sentence often begins with its subject, which generally captures old information from a preceding sentence. For example:

> e.g. 54. The defendant's lawyer was determined to break the prosecution's witness. She relentlessly cross-examined the stubborn witness for a week.

Here, "she" refers to "the defendant's lawyer", and both of them are human subjects. We can change the beginning of the second sentence to add some diversity. For example:

> e.g. 55. Relentlessly, she cross-examined the stubborn witness for a week. / For a week, she relentlessly cross-examined the stubborn witness. / Relentlessly, for a week, she cross-examined the stubborn witness.

Adverbs modify verbs, adjectives, other adverbs, or a whole clause. They can be almost at any place in a sentence. The adverbs at the beginning have also got emphasized.

Besides, in English, placing certain adverb modifiers at the beginning of a sentence requires you to change the normal subject-verb order as well. The most common of these modifiers are negatives, including "seldom" "hardly" "rarely" "in no case" and "not until". We should pay special attention to this sentence structure. For example:

> e.g. 56. Hardly we see such an honest man like you.

Example 56 is wrong. We need to reverse the subject and the verb as follows:

> e.g. 57. Hardly do we see such an honest man like you.

Tip 3: Combine types of sentences.

Most written sentences make statements. Occasionally, however, questions, commands or exclamations may enhance variety. Questions may set the direction of a paragraph and draw readers' attention. More often, the questions used in exposition or argument do not require answers but ideas that readers can be expected to agree with. Such questions are called rhetorical questions, just as the very famous sentence written by Shelley in *Ode to the West Wind*:

> e.g. 58. If winter comes, can spring be far behind?

Commands often occur in an explanation of a process, particularly in directions. Exclamations may add some of the author's feelings into the writing, which makes the writing more personal and vivid.

However, we should not vary sentences for the sake of varying. Variety occurs because a particular sentence type is effective for the context, not because the author sets out to achieve variety for its own sake.

 Exercises

I. Mark true (T) or false (F) for the following statements.

1. Any pronoun used in a context should have a clear antecedent. (　)

2. Concise language refers to simple but clear language. (　)

3. Imperative mood is more effective in giving directions. (　)

4. Syntactic variety mainly addresses the length of a sentence. (　)

5. The consistency in person usually involves the use of pronouns. (　)

6. Rhetorical questions ask for answers. (　)

7. Concise language and specific language are almost the same. (　)

8. The voice of a sentence includes the active voice and the passive voice. (　)

II. Revise the following sentences to make them clearer in meaning.

1. Melissa found a book in the antique case that her father had left for her.

Revised: _____

_____

2. Be brave to investigate, and you should also be careful to conclude.

Revised: _____

_____

3. The students were thrilled to know they will not have mid-term exams.

Revised: _____

_____

4. If you keep running every day, the 800-meter running test will be passed.

Revised: _____

_____

III. Complete the paragraph with "he" "she" or "her".

Passage 1

Anna was one of these last girls at age seven, and her father helped to foster the ambivalent condition. (1) _____ treated (2) _____ like an adult—with respect, deference, and consideration—but somehow, simultaneously, (3) _____ managed to protect and preserve in (4) _____ the feeling that everything (5) _____ encountered in the world was a brand-new discovery, unique to (6) _____ own mind.

Passage 2

Now, for the first time since the early months of Facebook's debut as a public company, analysts are wondering if there's a ceiling to Facebook's potential, and whether (7) _____ could hit the ceiling sooner rather than later. (8) _____ is stuck in a seeming rut, unsure how to keep (9) _____ ad business growing at a fast pace and how to pick which products (10) _____ should focus on.

IV. Decide whether the following sentences are concise (C) or wordy (W), and revise the wordy sentences.

1. The bird was purple, red, orange, and yellow in color, and its body was extremely large in size.

(C□ W□)

_____

_____

2. Controlling the quality and level of the television shows that children watch is a continuing challenge to parents that they must meet on a daily basis.

(C□ W□)

_____

_____

3. A large number of people are now seeking out various electronic devices as presents to give to others on their birthdays.

(C□ W□)

_____

_____

4. In 1962, Linus Pauling, who was an American, was awarded the Nobel Prize, which was given to him for his attempts to limit the making of nuclear arms and to curtail the spread of nuclear testing.

(C☐ W☐)

_____

_____

5. I found out recently that Benito Mussolini (1883–1945), the dictator of the fascist nation of Italy for a period lasting nearly twenty-one years, was named after the Mexican political leader who went by the name of Benito Juarez (1806–1872).

(C☐ W☐)

_____

_____

6. In today's uncertain economic climate, it is clear that people, namely, average middle-class working people, have great difficulty saving much money or putting anything aside for emergencies.

(C☐ W☐)

_____

_____

7. We thought the television program that was on last night was enjoyable, whereas our parents reacted with dislike to the content of the show.

(C☐ W☐)

_____

_____

8. Because of the bad weather, the school district felt it would be safer to cancel classes and let everyone stay home than to risk people having accidents on the way to school.

(C☐ W☐)

_____

_____

9. In this paper, I am planning to describe the hobby that I enjoy of collecting old comic books.

(C☐ W☐)

_____

_____

10. In Ben's opinion, he thinks that cable television will change and alter our lives in the future.

(C☐ W☐)

_____

_____

V. Decide whether the following sentences achieve consistency or not.

1. In May, unemployment fell to 3.8 percent—its lowest level in nearly 50 years.

(☐Yes ☐No)

2. Optimism among employers, particularly manufacturers and small businesses, have reached historic highs in the 6 months since tax reform became law.

(☐Yes ☐No)

3. Many economists expect the winning streak to continue, predicting second quarter GDP growth to exceed 4 percent.

(☐Yes ☐No)

4. This high-energy growth environment present both a challenge and an opportunity.

(☐Yes ☐No)

5. The challenge is that companies must find more workers with specific skill sets to fill an increasing number of open jobs.

(☐Yes ☐No)

6. The opportunity is that with more affordable, relevant training, many American workers would now have the chance to move into better jobs that deliver bigger paychecks.

(☐Yes ☐No)

VI. Read the following introduction to university missions, and discuss the syntactical variety in each introduction.

1. Cornell

Mission

Learning. Discovery. Engagement.

Cornell is a private, Ivy League university and the land-grant university for New York state. Cornell's mission is to discover, preserve and disseminate knowledge, to educate the next generation of global citizens, and to promote a culture of broad inquiry throughout and beyond the Cornell community. Cornell also aims, through public service, to enhance the lives and livelihoods of students, the people of New York and others around the world.

Vision

Cornell aspires to be the exemplary comprehensive research university for the 21st century. Faculty, staff and students thrive at Cornell because of its unparalleled combination of quality and breadth; its open, collaborative and innovative culture; its founding commitment to diversity and inclusion; its vibrant rural and urban campuses; and its land-grant legacy of public engagement.

2. MIT

Mission

The mission of MIT is to advance knowledge and educate students in science, technology, and other areas of scholarship that will best serve the nation and the world in the 21st century.

The Institute is committed to generating, disseminating, and preserving knowledge, and to working with others to bring this knowledge to bear on the world's great challenges. MIT is dedicated to providing its students with an education that combines rigorous academic study and the excitement of discovery with the support and intellectual stimulation of a diverse campus community. We seek to develop in each member of the MIT community the ability and passion to work wisely, creatively, and effectively for the betterment of humankind.

MIT's motto is "mens et manus", or "mind and hand", signifying the fusion of academic knowledge with practical purpose.

3. Brown

Mission

The mission of Brown University is to serve the community, the nation, and the world by discovering, communicating, and preserving knowledge and understanding in a spirit of free

inquiry, and by educating and preparing students to discharge the offices of life with usefulness and reputation. We do this through a partnership of students and teachers in a unified community known as a university-college.

Unit 3
Essay Development (I)

What makes it difficult to write an English essay? Adequate knowledge in grammar and vocabulary seems not a guarantee of developing a satisfactory essay. Are there any rules to follow? What are common patterns of essay development? What is an effective thesis statement? What details should be included in descriptive passages? What makes good narration? Is story-telling equal to a simple act of recounting events? Some simple yet effective writing techniques are to be introduced in this unit to help us write with confidence in English.

 ## Sensory Details

Lead-in Questions:

1. Why are sensory details important in descriptive writing?

2. What determines the choice of sensory details?

e.g. 1. "Sitting restlessly, this person couldn't help but peeling the skin at the edge of his thumb. This person thought everyone must have heard his heart pounding. The person rubbed the sweaty hands against knees, but failed to steady the shaking legs."

Who is being described in the picture? It must be the man on the right of the picture, right? If you're asked to think of one word to describe him, what would be the word? "Nervous" would probably be the first word that came to your mind. There are some details in the

description about the man's nervousness, such as "sitting restlessly" "peeling the skin" "heard his heart pounding" "rubbed the sweaty hands" and "shaking legs".

Now let's take a closer look at the details. "Sitting restlessly" "peeling the skin" "rubbed the hands" and "steady the shaking legs" are all about what you see. "Heard his heart pounding" is about what you hear. "Sweaty hands" is about what you feel. Seeing, hearing, feeling, smelling and tasting are the five senses of human being.

Good description is all about details—sensory details in particular. Suppose the three persons in the picture on the previous page are waiting for a job interview. If you say the man on the right was nervous, do you have a word for the man in the middle? Maybe it could be "impatient", and let us think of some sensory details to describe him as an impatient interviewee. We can begin with what we see:

e.g. 2. "He was kept waiting the whole morning. He repeatedly checked the time. It was lunch time and he could hear his stomach rumbling."

From the sensory details, we can tell the man was impatient. Now let's use sensory details to describe the lady on the left. Compared with the guys, she looked like a more relaxed interviewee. Again, we can begin with what we see:

e.g. 3. "She thought she would surely get the job. She sat cross-legged on the couch. She hummed a tune of Rihanna. A perfume of rose hung around her."

All the sensory details are telling us that the lady was relaxed. This is how we develop good description in English. We think of as many sensory details as we can to create an image and leave a dominant impression on our readers. Now let us look at another picture.

What is your impression of the library? It could be crowded. So let's think of some sensory details about the library. We can always begin with what we see. "The library is crowded and there is barely any vacancy. Students are busy studying. They have their eyes on books and screens." And then we try to imagine what students feel in the picture. "Students are working so hard. They have a sore neck. They are so concentrated on reading that when they take a break and look above, they feel the light blazing." Now let's imagine what people hear in the picture. "Although a library is supposed to be really quiet or simply because it is very quiet, when students are busy reading books, we can hear pages rustling. When people discuss questions with their partners, they have to whisper. But somehow, the neighbors feel disturbed and they shush the person." Let's move on to the rest two senses—smelling and tasting. "People usually smell coffee, newly-brewed coffee and there's always the smell of ink, fresh ink." But it seems that we don't taste anything in a library, right? Maybe we can use a rhetoric device. "Students taste the sweetness of knowledge." Finally, we organize all the sensory details and develop a paragraph as follows:

> e.g. 4. "There is barely any vacancy in the library. Students are busy studying with their eyes on books and screens. They work so hard and have to rub their sore necks from time to time. When they occasionally take a break and look above, they feel the blazing light. To stay refreshed and concentrated, a student is enjoying a cup of newly-brewed coffee. Although a library is supposed to be really quiet or simply because it is very quiet, when students are busy reading books, we can hear pages rustling. When people discuss questions with their partners, they have to whisper. But somehow, the neighbors feel disturbed and they shush the person."

You may have noticed we selected details that help create a dominant impression and omitted the rest of them. It's actually the dominant impression that determines details. The dominant impression we want to create determines what sensory details we select. Then we rearrange the details to make a complete paragraph. To employ sensory details in descriptive paragraphs is like to paint a picture to the readers because it can help visualize the situation and make vivid description. Readers can thereby be better engaged.

Comparison and Contrast

Lead-in Questions:

1. What are the two common patterns of organizing comparison and contrast?

2. What are the steps we are supposed to follow in organizing comparison and contrast?

Every day, one of the most frequent mental exercises we do, perhaps, is comparison and

contrast. For example, we may have to decide how to get to the classroom, because it takes about 20 minutes on foot, or 10 minutes by bike. We must compare the two choices. Or we may have to choose between a pair of comfortable sneakers and a pair of fashionable high-heels. In class, we must decide which professor's course we want to take. Upon graduation, we must decide whether to further our study or to take a full-time job. Likewise, using comparison and contrast is also one common way of developing a paragraph. In this section, we're going to focus on techniques in comparison and contrast.

Which one is your favorite mobile phone application, QQ or WeChat? Some of you may choose WeChat because it's easier to use. One of your friends just posted some photos and stories on WeChat, and you don't want to be left out and the last person to know. But some of you may choose QQ because your friends only use QQ and some of the group chat features work really well for college students. So how do you compare these two mobile applications and convince each other?

We can begin with brainstorming as many points of information as we can. First, ask yourself: What is the purpose of the comparison or contrast? Probably, the purpose is to make a judgment. This could also be the thesis of your essay, "Compared with WeChat, QQ is a better mobile application for college students."

The second question you want to ask yourself is: In what ways are these two applications similar and different? For example, we can compare the main features. There are common features both applications have, such as "instant messaging" "voice message" "facetime talk" "moments" "documents sharing", etc. For the common features, we can think about which one is easier to use.

Also, is there any feature that one has while the other one doesn't? There is Official Account in WeChat while there isn't in QQ. Although QQ has QQ Wallet, WeChat Pay is much more popular among businesses and customers and provides better financial services. People can pay in many stores and they can pay utilities bills with WeChat Pay. Besides, there is a feature called city services on WeChat, and people can make doctor appointments and pay traffic fines. Both QQ and WeChat have group chats, but we can do way much more things with QQ groups, such as online vote and document sharing. Some might say there is the invisible chat feature which is unique to QQ, with which people can talk in a group without showing their ID.

As you can see, there could be a very long list of similarities and differences, all of which can be strong supporting details of the thesis, "Compared with WeChat, QQ is a better mobile application for college students." But we can never persuade our readers with the details randomly listed as above, we need to organize them. There are two common patterns of organizing comparison and contrast in paragraphs and essays.

The first one is the "point-by-point" pattern. We compare or contrast the two applications on one point in each paragraph. As you see here, our thesis comes first. And in the first body paragraph, we compare the two applications on point one. In the second body paragraph, we compare the two apps on point two. And in the third paragraph, on point three. Finally, we come to a natural conclusion.

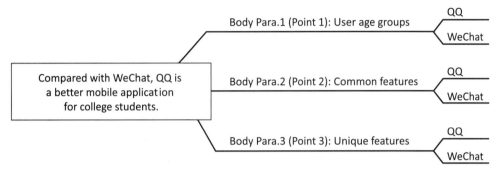

Figure 3–1   Point-by-point Pattern

There are two things we need to pay attention to in this pattern. First, be sure in each paragraph, we discuss the same subject first. Second, don't forget transitional expressions like "in contrast" "similarly" and "conversely", otherwise the paragraph would look like a pure verbal description of a graph.

The second pattern of organizing comparison and contrast is the "side-by-side" pattern. Again, we need to begin with a clear thesis statement. Then, in this pattern, we focus on one application first and discuss different points in one paragraph. In the second paragraph, we move on to the other application and discuss different points.

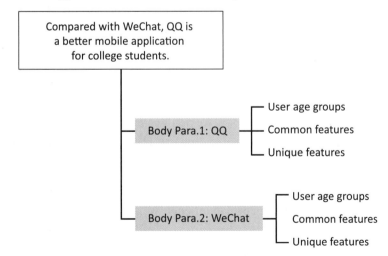

Figure 3–2   Side-by-side Pattern

Also, there are two things we need to be careful in this pattern. First, we need to compare the two subjects on each point in the same order. Second, since in this pattern two subjects are

discussed in two separate paragraphs, don't forget to refer to the other subject from time to time. Otherwise, readers may forget the other subject we talked about. Also, some connecting devices may be helpful.

Now that we have enough knowledge on comparison and contrast, let's work on a very familiar topic, pets. First, let's take a look at the passage below and see if you agree with the author.

> e.g. 5. Dogs are better company than cats. You can take them for walks, play games with them, talk to them, or teach them tricks. When you're depressed, it's nice to have someone around that you can count on to be loving and affectionate. Dogs are great for cheering people up. On the other hand, you can't do a lot with cats. They're mainly into sleeping and eating. They'll chase a piece of string you pull across the floor for a while, but it's the string that interests them more than you. Cats are mainly interested in themselves, while dogs get a lot of pleasure from people.

In the passage above, the author follows a side-by-side pattern. He/she talks about dogs in the first half, and cats in the second half. But probably, there are another one or two paragraphs developed in the same way, so the whole essay is a point-by-point pattern. How do we decide which pattern to use in our essay? If we want to present the bigger pictures of two subjects, we may follow the side-by-side pattern. For example, if we want to compare and contrast the first English presentation we did as a freshman and a presentation we did in our senior year, we may want to give readers an overview of the past situation first, and then the improvement we've achieved in marked contrast. But if our purpose is to show the audience that they should choose one subject over the other, we may follow the point-to-point pattern, because they want to know the advantages of one over the other.

When we intend to develop an essay or paragraph by comparison and contrast, we should begin by asking ourselves the purpose of it. We don't compare only for the sake of comparing. There must be a point to make. Don't just say "they're similar" or "they're different". If we're clear of our purpose, we have a clear thesis. Then we brainstorm as many points of information as possible, and put them in a table. The next thing is to decide a pattern we want to follow. Usually, in short essays, we stick to one pattern only. We should never forget to check if using proper transitions to connect ideas.

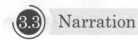 Narration

Lead-in Questions:

1. What is narration?

2. How can we tell a good story?

Human beings have a passion for stories. Remember when you were a kid, adults seemed to have endless stories to share over dinner? Every night, a bedtime story was the only reason for you to give up toys. Feeling alone in a party? Just raise your voice and say: "You know, something really weird happened to me last night!" Everyone would surely turn around. Everyone loves to listen to stories. Everyone loves to tell stories. Narration is to give an account of events, or simply, story-telling. What makes good story-telling? This section is about some essential story-telling techniques.

How do you like the following story?

> e.g. 6. Cynthia is just an ordinary girl in college. She is serious about her studies and has managed to meet all the deadlines. She gets along well with her roommates. She cares about her body and goes to the gym as much as she can.

It seems like an ordinary story that might happen every day, right? Even if a turning point is yet to come, the audience might have lost patience at the moment. What about the following passage?

> e.g. 7. When Nina saw the police car in front of Mrs. Wellington, a next-door neighbor, she ran to the house. Mrs. Wellington was like another grandmother to both Nina and Max. Nina specifically loved her neighbor's overflowing flower garden. Everyone did. The whole neighborhood looked forward to Mrs. Wellington's annual garden party, which was coming up again soon. That is, if everything was all right.

I believe you must have tons of questions at the moment. What went wrong? A police car? Was someone killed? Was it Mrs. Wellington? You must be curious about what has happened and eager to read on. This is a very arresting opening scene, which makes an important element in good story-telling. An opening scene should use as few sentences as possible to introduce the main characters, the background, and preferably, the conflict. In the passage above, the characters are Nina, Mrs. Wellington, and Max. Let's look for some clues about the background in the following sentences. "Mrs. Wellington was like another grandmother." "Everyone loved her garden." "The whole neighborhood looked forward to…" It seems that

Mrs. Wellington was a nice person and easy to get along with. But the police car looks so out of place against the background.

Let's take a look at another opening paragraph:

> e.g. 8. Six responsible adults. Three cute kids. One yapping dog. It's a quiet Sunday afternoon in the suburbs. What could possibly go wrong?

There are the characters. It gives audience the background. Adults are responsible, kids are cute, and it is a normal weekend. And obviously, the conflict is that something went wrong. Let's revise the passage about Cynthia and make the opening more arresting as follows:

> e.g. 9. She is serious about her studies and has managed to meet all the deadlines. She gets along well with her roommates. She cares about her body and goes to the gym as much as she can. Cynthia is just an ordinary girl in college. But what had happened to her last summer could be no more extraordinary.

Now that we have a good beginning, the next thing we do is to develop a timeline of events. Make a list of the major events in the story. Remember, we need to decide what to include in our story. We should save the most significant and unusual events, and ignore the unimportant ordinary details. Everyone knows the Titanic story. Look at the timeline of the events below:

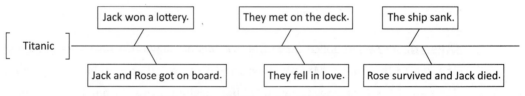

Figure 3–3   Timeline of the Titanic Story

With the timeline of events ready, the next thing we do is to decide the order of events. Of course, we can tell the story in the chronological order, which is the time order the events occur. But more often than not, people use flashbacks. The author tells audience certain crisis first, and then go back to tell them what has happened, like in most detective stories where there was always a body found in the first scene.

Now we have the events ready, and have decided an order, we need to collect some details for describing the events. Remember to include some sensory details that are especially expressive in descriptive writing. The next thing to do before we begin writing is to decide a point of view. We can tell a story from a third-person point of view or a first-person point of view. A first-person point of view is more direct, and sometimes unspoken thoughts can be directly conveyed. And a third-person point of view sometimes shows a different picture, or a different side of the story.

To sum up, we begin with an arresting opening scene. Then we develop a timeline with only the most important and exciting events. When we have a timeline, we decide an order. Then we collect some sensory details for description in the story and we pick a point of view.

Thesis Statement

Lead-in Questions:

1. What is a thesis statement?

2. How can we make a strong thesis statement?

In persuasive writing, when you have a topic to write about—be it given as a writing assignment or one that you have been wanting to write about for a while—and have a target audience in mind, you might want to begin the writing process with a thesis statement.

An effective thesis statement is very important to help develop a persuasive essay. The thesis statement is one or two sentences summarizing the main point or the controlling idea of your essay. It gives the following information to the audience: first, the subject of the essay; second, the writer's opinion on the subject. Also, remember to put your thesis statement in the first paragraph of your essay. Unlike Chinese readers, English readers like to know exactly what the essay is about at the beginning of the essay, not the end. Be aware of the big difference in essay writing in the two languages.

Let's look at the first paragraph of a student's essay:

e.g. 10. College students are required to take various courses to earn enough credits to graduate. Students can choose to take courses based on their interest and possible future career. Some courses are mandatory, and some are elective. Should students be required to take mandatory courses that are not relevant to their majors?

This is a very good beginning. It is concise and provides sufficient background information. But the thesis should be a statement. Usually, it's not a question. How about the following thesis statement?

e.g. 11. In this essay, I'm going to focus on some mandatory courses at college level.

This is a clear statement. The author tells audience the subject of the essay, "some mandatory courses", but fails to tell them his/her opinion and position on the issue. In a good thesis statement, you need to state clearly and specifically your opinion on the subject. What about the following version?

e.g. 12. The question of whether students should take mandatory courses that are not directly related to their majors has become a controversial issue.

Yes, it is a controversial issue. Still, what's your opinion on that issue? Let's continue to work on improving the thesis statement.

e.g. 13. In this essay, I want to give my opinion on whether students should take mandatory courses that are not directly related to their majors.

It is still not a good thesis statement, even if you say "I want to give my opinion…", because you fail to tell your audience what exactly is your opinion on this issue. Do you agree or disagree? Let's see what can be improved in the following thesis statement:

e.g. 14. Many students believe that mandatory courses at college level should be directly related to their majors. I tend to agree with some of them.

Compared with previous versions, the one above is definitely much better in that the author mentions the subject, and states his/her opinion on the issue. But, to develop an effective and strong thesis statement, we need to make it clear and specific. Try to avoid expressions like "I believe" and "in my opinion". Let's make final improvement to the thesis statement:

e.g. 15. College students are required to take various courses to earn enough credits to graduate. Students can choose to take courses based on their interest and possible future career. Some courses are mandatory, and some are elective. Mandatory courses should be directly related to their majors and students should be given the right to change their majors.

As you can see, this version looks very good except for one thing. Do you notice that the author tries to make two points in the thesis? Always remember to focus on only one point in one essay. "One thing at a time" is the golden rule. Let's delete the second point and we've got a very good introductory paragraph.

To sum up, in persuasive writing, a thesis statement is one or two sentences summarizing the main point/controlling idea of the thesis. It should cover two points: first, the subject of the essay; second, the author's opinion on the issue, i.e., his/her position. To develop a strong and effective thesis statement, we need to be direct and specific and focus on one idea only.

Exercises

I.　**Mark true (T) or false (F) for the following statements.**

1. To develop a good descriptive paragraph, it's necessary to include descriptive details about all the five senses.　(　　)

2. In descriptive writing, the author should have a dominant impression in mind and let it determine details.　(　　)

3. In an essay or a paragraph developed by comparison and contrast, the author should be clear of the purpose of comparing.　(　　)

4. In an essay or a paragraph developed by comparison and contrast, if the overall picture of each subject is to be emphasized, the author should follow the point-by-point pattern.

　(　　)

5. If the purpose is to present superiority or advantage of one subject over another, the author should adopt the side-by-side pattern.　(　　)

6. In good story-telling, it's reasonable to create an arresting opening scene.　(　　)

7. A chronological order in narration helps the author give an account of events so it's more desirable than any other narrative order.　(　　)

8. The thesis statement is usually found in the first paragraph of an essay.　(　　)

9. The thesis statement can be stated in the form of a question.　(　　)

10. A thesis statement is merely about the subject matter of the essay.　(　　)

II.　**Complete the following passage by choosing a proper word from the box to develop effective description.**

(a) accustomed	(b) propped	(c) vibrant	(d) squirm
(e) bent	(f) wriggle	(g) molded	

In none of her memories of him was Anna's father not saying something. He lived, in her memory, like a(n) (1) ＿＿＿＿＿＿ statue, (2) ＿＿＿＿＿＿ in the shape of his (3) ＿＿＿＿＿＿ listening posture: right knee (4) ＿＿＿＿＿＿ over the left, elbow (5) ＿＿＿＿＿ against the knee, his chin in his palm. He adopted this attitude

frequently, but even when so silently bound in attention, Anna's father couldn't help but communicate, and his lips and eyebrows would (6) _____ and (7) _____ in reaction to the things people said to him.

Ⅲ. **The following thesis statements are ineffective. Identify the problem with each statement and rewrite it to make it clearer and more effective.**

1. In this essay, I'm going to talk about elective courses for English majors.

   The thesis statement is not effective because _____ .

   A better version could be _____ .

2. Diseases have been affecting human beings in many ways.

   The thesis statement is not effective because _____ .

   A better version could be _____ .

3. Cyber-bullying is a terrible problem.

   The thesis statement is not effective because _____ .

   A better version could be _____ .

4. GPA is an important indicator of academic success but not of one's character.

   The thesis statement is not effective because _____ .

   A better version could be _____ .

5. I tend to believe people have been alienated by the Internet.

   The thesis statement is not effective because _____ .

   A better version could be _____ .

IV. **Match the sentences (a)–(c) with (1)–(3) and develop a paragraph with the point–by–point pattern.**

(a) Modern Western medicine treats individual bodies as instances of universal laws of nature as studied by science.

(b) In the West, the focus on individuals has led to the widespread influence of Psychology as a proliferating discipline, first for treating mental illness, then for predicting how individuals are likely to act, in their personal motivations and in their buying habits.

(c) Under modernity Westerners have tended to play down the importance of group phenomena that are studied by sociologists, such as clan, class, or society.

(1) These are precisely the concerns that have remained dominant in Chinese civilization. The West has tended to invest more attention in psychology, focused on people taken one at a time.

(2) Traditional Chinese medicine, by contrast, uses a vocabulary of *qi* energy to describe the specific state of *qi*-energy flow in each patient.

(3) The Chinese habitually start from concern for groups and the way humans should fit into them. This is why face is such an important factor in Chinese life.

Unit 4
Essay Development (II)

This unit continues to explore important topics in essay development. In exposition and argumentation, two major patterns of English essay development, supporting details must be included to make a strong thesis. What are common types of supporting details? Are there any rules to select and organize valid supporting details? People always say a good beginning is half the battle won. What are the options to make an impressive and strong opening paragraph? Is catching attention the goal to achieve in a good introduction? How about the ending paragraph? What must be included? When we finish the unit, we will have a good sense of developing effective essays.

Supporting Details

Lead-in Questions:

1. What makes a strong argument?

2. Evidence alone does not make a strong argument. What else do we need?

Do you remember the idea of "thesis statement" mentioned in the previous unit? It is one or two sentences summarizing the main point or the controlling idea of your essay. Let's look at the following thesis:

e.g. 1. Since last semester, takeout food has become a trend on our campus. Students are given more choices as to what and when to eat. But the service has been banned recently. We hold that takeout food service from off-campus providers should be allowed.

The thesis statement above is clear and effective in that it gives the following information to audience: first, the subject of the essay; second, the writer's opinion on the subject. What do we do next? We need supporting details. A clear thesis statement plus enough supporting details makes a strong argument. Let's make a list of evidence to support the thesis.

- more choices of food
- more freedom of when to eat

• cheaper than cafeteria food   • saving time

...

In English argumentative writing, there are many different kinds of evidence we can present to support our thesis statement. The easiest way of research is to go online and look for possible evidence.

Facts and statistics can serve as supporting evidence. The following is what a student finds online. "According to a recent survey conducted by the Students' Union, more than 80% of the students ordered takeout food service at least once in the past month." As we can see, 80% is a popular majority. Here's another piece of evidence found online. "A diversity of food choice undoubtedly helps people maintain a balanced diet, stated the Director of the Health Department of the university clinic." In this one, we're quoting the Director of the Health Department. These are some specific words from knowledgeable people in certain field to support our idea. So, quotations are also a common type of supporting evidence. Let's look at another example:

e.g. 2. An official report from "China Consumers Association" showed that more than half of college students prefer takeout food over cafeteria food if they are given the choice.

The evidence above includes not only numbers, but also authoritative references from experts and official studies. In our argumentation, we can use them as supporting details. Apart from statistics, quotations, and reference to official studies, we can turn to personal experience for more varied types of evidence. For example:

e.g. 3. Last Friday, it was almost midnight after a long day of work in the lab. Nasir felt exhausted and the cafeteria was closed. He ordered food online before he left for his dorm. When he got there, the food was on his desk, warm and ready. "Takeout food delivery seems to me the only choice when cafeteria opening hours don't work for me."

It's a personal story, but it helps to prove that takeout food is a very good choice when cafeteria food is not available.

It seems that we have collected enough supporting evidence for the thesis. But argumentation isn't just about searching for evidence. Supporting details can be in other forms, such as definition and explanation. Sometimes, before we present supporting evidence, we need to define and explain one or two key terms in our thesis statement so that the discussion is

limited and manageable. Let's ask ourselves if there is anything we need to define in the thesis statement—"We hold that takeout food service from off-campus providers should be banned." What is the background? What do you mean by "off-campus providers"? So, we can give the following explanation:

> e.g. 4. In most universities in China, students are encouraged to go to the cafeterias on campus for many reasons. It's the most convenient and food safety is guaranteed. But now students can order food online and have it delivered. The takeout food is neither processed nor delivered by the university cafeteria. Despite its popularity, the service was banned last month.

The paragraph above gives background information about the topic. When we argue for a point, we need to explain the situation so as to limit our discussion to a manageable scope, and then provide supporting evidence. In this topic, we also need to explain why there is such a ban. For example:

> e.g. 5. Last month, the university administration issued a ban on food delivery service from off-campus providers, mainly for food safety reasons. There have already been several cases of food poisoning reported on campus in the past month.

As we can see, there were cases of food poisoning and the university was concerned about food safety on campus. After we explain the reason, we're actually better prepared to analyze the problem and argue for our point. Sometimes, reason analysis is also necessary in argumentative writing. Instead of directly jumping to supporting evidence, we can actually make a more complete and stronger case by analyzing reasons. This is all part of the whole argumentation process.

Let's look at another example. At the beginning of the unit, one of the reasons we come up with is that takeout food means more freedom of when to eat. We can explain it in detail and analyze why we can't do this in the cafeteria. The following is from a student's writing, in which a very detailed analysis of the situation is made.

> e.g. 6. All the cafeterias on campus have regular opening hours, which means we can have food only when they're open. You can imagine the crowd during rush hours, since we have almost the same class schedules. Unlike cafeterias, off-campus restaurants are open 24/7. I can order a bottle of soy milk at 10 a.m. on weekend mornings, and I can also order a slice of cheesecake at 3 p.m. to enjoy when I take a break. The best experience is that it can be delivered to anywhere on campus, my room, the classroom, the lab, or the gym.

From the examples above, we can see argumentation is not just about presenting as much supporting evidence as we can. Supporting evidence alone doesn't make a strong argument. We need analysis and explanations to piece them together.

To sum up, in argumentative writing, we begin with a clear thesis statement. The next thing to do is to think about supporting details. There are various types of supporting details, including facts and statistics, references to authoritative studies and research, quotations from knowledgeable people, personal stories or anecdotes, etc. Evidence alone doesn't make a strong argument. When we have it ready, we need to come up with ways to piece together all the supporting evidence. To begin with, we need to define the topic so as to limit our discussion to certain aspects. Definitions and explanations are both necessary to set the background of the discussion. Sometimes, we need to analyze the situation in full details so that readers are clear of reasons and impact. We call it "reason analysis".

 Introductions and Conclusions (I)

Lead-in Questions:

1. How can we turn our introductions into attention grabbers?

2. What should be included in the introduction of an essay?

Suppose you're given a writing prompt on the argument that "Online learning will replace traditional classroom learning in the future". How would you begin your essay?

e.g. 7. With the development of technology, online learning has become more and more popular...

It looks like a very familiar beginning to you, doesn't it? It is a very common lead-in sentence, but it's just not interesting enough to grab readers' attention. In this section, let's focus on dos and don'ts of lead-ins in introductions.

Tip 1: Make the lead-ins grabbers.

Some lead-ins are indeed too common to use. You know there's a joke. If English teachers were given a dollar for every essay that begins with "With the development of science and technology...", they could all retire to Phuket Island. There are many ways to grab readers' attention. For example, we may want to begin with shocking statistics as follows:

e.g. 8. One of every three students on campus reportedly have experience in online learning, and one of every ten of them have received certificate of online courses, according to a recent survey conducted by the Students' Union.

Although online learning is no news to most people, the numbers above still give readers some concrete evidence as to how popular it has become. So, this is a good attention-grabber. Let's look at another example:

> e.g. 9. When Einstein wrote that the "most beautiful thing we can experience is the mysterious", I don't believe he was thinking about the mystery smell coming from our attic last summer.

"Mystery smell coming from our attic" sounds like a detective story, right? The author uses a quotation from a historical figure, though in a humorous way. Speaking of quotation, we can also begin with memorable proverbs or traditional sayings. But don't overuse them. Proverbs like "A coin has two sides" are overused so we might want to avoid them. Apart from proverbs and quotations, sometimes people like to use a paradox. For example, in an essay about depression, the beginning goes in this way:

> e.g. 10. "Eat two chocolate bars and call me in the morning," says the psychiatrist to the patient. Such advice sounds like a sugar fanatic's dream, but recent studies have indeed confirmed that chocolate positively affects depression and anxiety.

Eating chocolate to combat depression indeed sounds like an impossible fact or a paradox. Common facts are just not interesting enough, and that's why some authors like to begin with a paradox or uncommon facts.

Sometimes experienced writers like to present a startling claim so as to attract all the attention, just like in the following essay beginning:

> e.g. 11. In the future, all translators will be unemployed because computers will be smart enough to do accurate translation.

This is a very intriguing and startling claim, and readers want to read to find out why. But when you make a bold statement like this, be sure you are very confident to make a convincing case. Speaking of boldness, there's an essay that begins like this:

> e.g. 12. "Be bold! You can do it!" said my roommate again and again, during the weeks before choir tryouts, despite my whimpering cries of "I can't, I can't". For a shy person like me, the thought of singing in a public audition was agony. But thanks to the ABC Relaxation Method suggested by the Counseling Center, I performed so well I was chosen for a solo. The method, incorporating visualization and proper breathing techniques, is a helpful process every shy person should practice regularly.

A conversation that happens between friends like in Example 12 makes an anecdote, or a personal experience. The conversation could also be a good beginning which your audience can easily relate to.

Tip 2: Keep the lead-ins brief.

We must keep the lead-ins brief, especially in short essays. Remember that the lead-ins act only as hooks to attract attention and we don't want the introductions to turn out to be the major parts of our essays. Let's read another essay beginning:

e.g. 13. With one eye blackened, one arm in a cast, and third-degree burn on both her legs, the pretty, blond two-year-old seeks corners of rooms, refuses to speak, and shakes violently at the sound of loud noises. Tammy is not the victim of a war or a natural disaster; rather, she is the helpless victim of her parents, one of the thousands of children who suffer daily from American's hidden crime.

The essay is about child abuse and the author begins with a detailed description of the victim of the crime. This helps to emotionally involve readers in the situation.

With all the examples of intriguing and effective essay beginnings, we get back to our writing assignment about online learning. What could be a good topic lead-in for this assignment? As we're supposed to talk about a future trend in contrast to a traditional situation, why not try a contrast, or a before-v.s.-after scenario? The following is a comparison between the two situations:

e.g. 14. I used to be the first one to show up in the classroom just to get the best seat. I used to miss excellent lectures because there's a conflict of schedule. But all that has changed! Now I can choose when and where to learn. Attending online classes has transformed the way I explore the world.

This is so much better than the lead-in "with the development...". Example 14 presents a very sharp contrast. Similarly, we can make a comparison, or an analogy, to begin with something the readers are already very familiar with, as shown in Example 15:

e.g. 15. When the first Kindle came out, not many readers would prefer it over the fresh smell of ink. But now most of them read on their Kindles while studying online courses on their mobile phones.

As we can see, this is a good analogy of how technology has changed the way people learn and read. Speaking of changes, there are always some doubts or popular misconceptions, which could also be good lead-ins. For example:

e.g. 16. Some people value communication in the learning process and they believe online learning lacks the exact essence of learning, communication. But this has changed when live online communication was included in most online courses.

To sum up, we discussed many different types of lead-ins. There are shocking statistics, quotations, proverbs, a paradox, a startling claim, an anecdote, a detailed description, a contrast, an analogy, and popular misconceptions.

There are also some rules about lead-ins. First, make the lead-ins attention grabbers. Don't begin by saying "with the development of…" anymore. Second, keep the lead-ins brief and don't make it the major parts of the essays. One last thing to mention is that only the lead-ins do not make complete introductions, and a thesis statement should also be included in the introduction.

 ## Introductions and Conclusions (II)

Lead-in Questions:

1. What makes a good introduction?

2. How can we write a good conclusion?

Now we're given a writing prompt on the argument that "to live in a foreign country is the best way to learn a foreign language", and we may develop an introductory paragraph as follows:

e.g. 17. I've been learning English for more than ten years. Still, I have to struggle with what to say. It's been a nightmare. Until last year, I participated in an exchange program and stayed in Chicago for three months, and I began to feel confident to speak English for the first time in my life. In this essay, I want to talk about my experience of learning a foreign language.

The audience would be interested in reading the experience, which makes it a good beginning. Where's the thesis statement in Example 17? Is it a good thesis statement? Not really. It only tells the audience the subject matter of the essay, which does not equal an effective thesis statement. Let's take a look at another lead-in paragraph on the same topic:

e.g. 18. One can never grasp a foreign language until he forgets his native language, according to a language expert. The mission seems impossible, yet it may be achieved through living in a foreign country, when one's native language is somewhat forgotten temporarily. In this sense, to live in a foreign country is the best way to learn a foreign language.

How can anyone forget one's mother tongue? It looks like a paradox, doesn't it? At least, there's a bit of exaggeration in the claim. But this is a very impressive lead-in and the audience would probably like to read on and find out how. You must have also noticed the last sentence as the thesis statement. So, an impressive lead-in plus a specific thesis makes this version an excellent example of introduction.

Next, let's take a look at the idea of "essay map". Do you remember your first year as a freshmen student? Maybe you can relate to the following paragraph:

> e.g. 19. College is designed to be a time of personal growth and expansion. Yet many freshmen students find it hard to adapt to the new life and struggle with their studies. The practice of Senior Counselors is an excellent idea for first-year students to receive help in many ways. Their help makes a world of difference because they serve as liaisons between students and professors, experienced tutors, and life coaches.

Let's first identify the lead-in and thesis statement in this introductory paragraph. The first two sentences are the lead-in part. The author's thesis statement is in the middle. "The practice of Senior Counselors is an excellent idea for first-year students to receive help in many ways." So, what about the last sentence? In the sentence, the author tells us the major points he/she is going to discuss in the essay, which is like a map showing us the direction.

Writing is like a trip the author takes together with the audience. His/her stand is like the destination. The author shows us the route we're going to take on the essay map. Therefore, we know in advance where we're headed. It gives us a brief yet specific idea about where the essay is going so that we will never get lost. Let's read the following sentences at the end of an introductory paragraph:

> e.g. 20. The library's reserve facility is badly managed. Its unpredictable hours, poor staffing, and inadequate space discourage even the most dedicated students.

In Example 20, the second sentence is the essay map, which always follows the thesis statement. Sometimes, however, the essay map may come before the thesis. Read the following paragraph and note the changes:

> e.g. 21. Because of their roles as liaisons between students and professors, experienced tutors, and life coaches, Senior Counselors made a world of difference in helping freshmen students adapt.

In Example 21, the essay map is the first part of the sentence and it comes before the thesis. We can make the sentence shorter and more concise as follows: "Unreasonable hours, poor staffing, and inadequate space make the library's reserve facility difficult to use." In this way, the essay map becomes part of the thesis statement. Let's take a look at the following paragraph:

e.g. 22. Senior Counselors are helpful for three reasons. The reasons are they serve as liaisons between students and professors, experienced tutors, and life coaches.

In Example 22, the author makes the essay map too obvious and mechanical, and we can change it into the following version. "Being liaisons between students and professors, experienced tutors, and life coaches, Senior Counselors play a major role in helping freshmen students adapt."

Before we move on to the conclusion, let's summarize what we have discussed about the introduction. A complete introduction consists of three parts, the lead-in, the thesis statement, and the essay map. We may find it really hard to work out a whole essay map in the beginning of the writing process, especially when there is a time limit like in exams. People may change directions from time to time. We can make an outline first, leave some space in the introduction and come back to finish it after we finish the main body. Maybe in the process, we come up with new ideas to use as a lead-in.

We're ready to move on to conclusion. Is conclusion simply about summarizing what has been said in previous paragraphs? Let's see if the following conclusion is proper for the introduction mentioned earlier, "Being liaisons between students and professors, experienced tutors, and life coaches, Senior Counselors play a major role in helping freshmen students adapt."

e.g. 23. In conclusion, the practice of Senior Counselors is an excellent idea because they are liaisons between students and professors, experienced tutors, and life coaches.

The author does a good job summarizing all the main points in the conclusion. But don't you find that the author uses almost the same words as in the introduction, like a simple copy? Rule 1 in conclusion is: Don't simply make a word-to-word copy of the thesis. Try to paraphrase it and reemphasize the thesis. Let's revise the conclusion above:

e.g. 24. In conclusion, Senior Counselors help college students to get well with professors, achieve academic success, make smarter choices in life and go through life crises together.

There are some obvious improvements in Example 24, because the author reemphasizes the major points through paraphrasing. But, do you notice that the author brings up a new point about "going through life crises"? There may be a little bit of exaggeration in the statement. Most importantly, this is a new point. Rule 2 in conclusion is: Don't bring up new points or new examples. Rule 3 is: Don't exaggerate or moralize your claim. Also, if possible, in your conclusion, you can try to echo your lead-in. So, you'd like to add a sentence to the conclusion to echo what has been mentioned in the introduction. For example:

e.g. 25. It's said that college is for young people to explore the world. As significant companions in the exploration, Senior Counselors help college students to get well with professors, achieve academic success and make smarter choices in life.

 ## 4.4 Body Paragraphs

Lead-in Questions:

1. What are the rules for a good topic sentence?

2. How can we achieve coherence in a paragraph?

In previous sections, we discussed how to work out an effective thesis statement and learned to present supporting details. In this section, we're going to focus on common errors in body paragraphs.

What makes a good paragraph? Some might say the topic sentence is one of the essential elements of a paragraph. First, it tells us what the paragraph is about. Second, it contributes a main point to support the thesis of the entire essay. Let's look at the thesis statement in Example 26 and think of a topic sentence of the body paragraph:

e.g. 26. The practice of Senior Counselors is an excellent idea for freshman students to receive help in many ways.

e.g. 27. Many students think that Senior Counselors play an important role.

Example 27 is too broad. What students? How important? What kind of role do they play? Rule 1 is: Topic sentences should be specific. We can revise it as follows: "Freshmen students think that Senior Counselors help them quickly adapt to the new life." The revised version is much more specific. Another example of the topic sentence goes like this:

e.g. 28. Senior Counselors offer tutoring to freshmen, which is also a rewarding experience to Counselors.

Example 28 is more specific. But do you note that there're two points in the statement? One is "offer tutoring" and the other is "a rewarding experience". Rule 2 is: Topic sentences should be focused on one point. It can be revised as follows: "Senior Counselors offer tutoring to freshmen to help them achieve academic success."

When we have a specific and focused topic sentence, we should also make sure all the sentences in the paragraph work to support this single point. In this way, all the "single points" in each paragraph work together to support the thesis statement. This is the first goal we try to achieve in a paragraph—unity.

Next, we can spend some time on coherence. In a coherent paragraph, ideas are stuck together so that they flow smoothly and logically. How do we achieve coherence? We need to decide an order. The supporting details should be organized in a logical order. Let's look at the following paragraph:

e.g. 29. At the first stage in the paper recycling process, waste paper is collected either from paper banks, where members of the public leave their used paper, or directly from businesses. This paper is then sorted by hand and separated according to its grade, with any paper that is not suitable for recycling being removed. Next, the graded paper is transported to a paper mill.

Example 29 is about the process of paper recycling and is developed in the order of time. Let's look at Example 30:

e.g. 30. He had some statuettes in his study. They stood on a high cupboard behind his desk. One was a lady wearing nothing but a bath towel. She seemed frozen in an eternal panic lest the bath towel slip down any farther, and since she had no arms, she was in an unfortunate position to pull the towel up again. Next to her, crouched the statuette of a leopard, ready to spring down at the top drawer of a filing cabinet. Beyond the leopard was a naked, muscular gentleman, who sat, looking down, with his chin on his fist and his elbow on his knee. He seemed utterly miserable.

Example 30 is developed in the order of space. The author writes like a camera moving from one statuette to another to present all the details. In most expository and argumentative paragraphs, people usually write in the next two patterns. Let's see another example:

e.g. 31. Ashura, one of the most important celebrations for Muslims, is a mixture of religious, cultural and traditional practices. It is celebrated on Muharram 10th every year. On this occasion, families meet together for a special meal of dried fruit. They also eat cakes and drink milk or juice. More importantly, they offer Zakat to poor people. Moreover, families and friends meet each other on the big day to play their drums while singing and dancing.

It seems that there is no particular order in Example 31, right? Do you notice the author begins with a general topic sentence and then provides details to support the general statement? We call it a deductive order. As authors, we move from a general statement to particular details. The opposite is the inductive order, in which we begin with specific details and end with a general statement. Example 32 is developed in an inductive order:

e.g. 32. When you are in middle school, the work gets harder. The amount of homework increases, and your parents give you more responsibilities because you are older. Even though you are older, you are still not old enough to drive or be out for long periods of time by yourself. You are in an uncomfortable space between being a teenager and being a little child. The middle school years are particularly difficult.

In the inductive pattern, the paragraph ends with the topic sentence. When we have a topic sentence, the first thing is to decide the order and stick to it throughout the whole paragraph, which is one technique to achieve coherence. There are some other simple tips. One is to use transitional expressions. Let's look at the underlined transitional expressions in Example 33:

e.g. 33. <u>At the first stage</u> in the paper recycling process, waste paper is collected either from paper banks, where members of the public leave their used paper, or directly from businesses. This paper is <u>then</u> sorted by hand and separated according to its grade, with any paper that is not suitable for recycling being removed. <u>Next</u>, the graded paper is transported to a paper mill.

Let's check for more transitional expressions about time order. Time signals include "first" "then" "next" "after" "as before" "while" "meanwhile" "soon" "now" "during" "finally" "after a while" "as soon as" "at that time" "by then" "since" "suddenly" "then" "thereafter" "by then" "by that time", and so on.

e.g. 34. He had some statuettes in his study. They stood <u>on a high cupboard behind his desk</u>. One was a lady wearing nothing but a bath towel. She seemed frozen in an eternal panic lest the bath towel slip down any farther, and since she had no arms, she was in an unfortunate position to pull the towel up again. <u>Next to her,</u>

crouched the statuette of a leopard, ready to spring down at the top drawer of a filing cabinet. <u>Beyond the leopard</u> was a naked, muscular gentleman, who sat, looking down, with his chin on his fist and his elbow on his knee. He seemed utterly miserable.

Let's check for more transitional expressions about space order. Space signals include "next to" "across" "on the opposite side" "to the left" "to the right" "above" "below" "near" "nearby" "besides" "on top of" "under" "over" "underneath" "far from", and so on.

There are also expressions indicating logic, such as "by contrast" "in addition" "consequently", etc. But not every sentence has to begin with transitional expressions. Use them only when necessary. Another technique to help achieve coherence is to repeat keywords or to use pronouns and synonyms. Let's take a look at Example 35 and try to identify all the techniques to achieve coherence.

e.g. 35. Transitions are the glue that holds a paragraph together. These devices lead the reader from sentence to sentence, smoothing over the gaps between by indicating the relationship between the sentences. If this glue is missing, the paragraph will almost inevitably sound choppy or childish, even if every sentence in it responds to a single topic commitment. However, transitions are not substitutes for topic unity: like most glue, they are most effective when joining similar objects, or, in this case, similar ideas. For example, in a paragraph describing a chicken egg, no transition could bridge the gap created by the inclusion of a sentence concerned with naval losses in the Civil War. In other words, transitions can call attention to the topic relationships between sentences, but they cannot create those relationships.

In this paragraph about "paragraphs", the topic sentence is obviously the first sentence. It's developed in a deductive order, with a general statement in the beginning. The keywords that are repeated several times are "transition" "glue", and "relationship". Sometimes, they are replaced by pronouns or synonyms, like "these devices" and "they". Some transitional devices are also found in the passage, including "however" "like most glue" "in this case" "for example", and "in other words". All the techniques mentioned above make the passage a very good example of a well-organized paragraph. It sticks to one point only, and provides sufficient details. Ideas are connected logically and smoothly.

 Exercises

I. Mark true (T) or false (F) for the following statements.

1. As long as we search for enough evidence, we can make a strong case in argumentative writing. ( )

2. Personal stories cannot be used as supporting details. ( )

3. In essay writing, it's necessary to limit the scope of discussion to a manageable case. ( )

4. It's acceptable to make a startling claim to attract attention in the beginning of an essay, as long as the author can make a convincing case. ( )

5. A few lead-in sentences help set the background of discussion. ( )

6. Statistics can only be used as supporting details but not essay beginnings. ( )

7. A sentence that serves as the essay map usually goes with the thesis statement to give audience a clearer picture of what the essay is about. ( )

8. In the conclusion of an essay, it's reasonable to bring up new examples to develop a strong argument. ( )

9. A topic sentence of a paragraph should contribute a main point to support the thesis of the entire essay. ( )

10. Transitional expressions indicate logic between sentences so they should be used before every sentence. ( )

II. The following are five thesis statements and a topic sentence (a) has been given for each statement. Add another topic sentence (b) to support the thesis.

1. College can be a challenging time for most students.

   a. Students find it hard to learn to be independent in everyday life.

   b. _____.

2. Swimming should be made a compulsory course in college.

   a. Swimming is an essential survival skill.

   b. _____.

3. Privately-run restaurants should be allowed on college campus.

    a. Students have more choices of food.

    b. _____ .

4. Cultural heritage sites should be made free for all visitors.

    a. The visit can be a valuable experience for people to know their own history.

    b. _____ .

5. Social distancing should be practiced in all public places.

    a. It's effective in preventing a public health crisis.

    b. _____ .

Ⅲ. **Develop two different introductions to the following claim: Overcoming procrastination is an effective strategy to meet a deadline.**

_____

_____

_____

_____

_____

_____

_____

_____

_____

_____

_____

_____

_____

_____

Unit 5
Rhetoric (I)

Rhetoric might be a new word to us, but it is not new at all in our life. For instance, a person annoys us. We start feeling upset, and we say: "Why don't you leave me alone?" By posing such a question, we do not ask for a reason. Instead, we simply want him/her to stop annoying us. In this case, we are using our language in a particular way for effective communication; in other words, we are making use of rhetoric. In this unit, we will grasp the basic concept of rhetoric, discuss how rhetoric can empower language, and learn to use some common rhetorical devices in writing.

 A Brief Introduction to Rhetoric and Rhetorical Devices

Lead-in Questions:

1. What is rhetoric as a technical term?

2. What are the three appeals in Aristotle's *Rhetoric*?

3. What are the classifications of rhetorical devices?

5.1.1 Rhetoric

Rhetoric may be used as an ordinary word or a technical term. As an ordinary word, it's commonly used to mean empty, inflated language or a misleading argument. However, when rhetoric is used as a technical term, it is about the skill or art of using language effectively. This unit focuses on rhetoric as a technical term.

The study of rhetoric goes back to ancient Greece. The word "rhetoric" is derived from the Greek word "rhetorike" which denotes the civic art of public speaking. In his book *Rhetoric*, Aristotle defined rhetoric as the art of persuasion. He identified three tools that public speakers could use to persuade an audience. He called them the appeals of ethos, pathos, and logos. As speakers can use them to appeal to the audience and win agreement, these three appeals are considered the most important in argumentation.

1. Ethos

Ethos is appeal based on the character of the speaker. It is the personal credibility, the faith people have in the speaker's identity. Ethos-driven writing relies on the reputation of the author.

2. Pathos

Pathos means persuading by appealing to the audience's emotions. People can think logically, but they also have emotions, and they are usually persuaded by emotional appeals. It means that they are in the emotion to trust another person's communication. Language choice affects the audience's emotional response, so emotional appeal can effectively be used to enhance an argument.

3. Logos

Logos means persuading by the use of reasoning. Logos is appeal based on logic or reason. Logos contains not only logic, but also facts, sufficient reasons and so on.

Aristotle's explanation on rhetoric has exerted a great influence on the development of the art of rhetoric, and Western education as well. In the *New Oxford Dictionary of English*, rhetoric is described as "the art of effective or persuasive speaking or writing, especially the exploitation of figures of speech or other compositional techniques".

5.1.2 Rhetorical Devices

The word "device" means a technique employed to achieve a particular effect, so rhetorical devices refer to specific techniques that a writer or a speaker uses to achieve a special effect or heighten the effect in expression. The English language also boasts a wide variety of rhetorical devices, while each one has its own form, characteristics, and peculiar way of achieving effect. Sometimes two or more devices can be used together for greater effect.

The magic of rhetorical devices can never be overstated. Rhetorical devices are like the color to a painting, making your speeches or essays more interesting and vivid. It can also help you to grasp and keep your readers' attention. Your language can be focused, clear, and concise, but without rhetorical devices, it still lacks vitality and glamor. Let's make a simple comparison. A black and white sketch might present a smiling woman, but without color, it's not Mona Lisa. Therefore, if you want to be a good writer, you can learn more about rhetorical devices and use them in writing. They are the very spices for dishes, without which the writings will fail to shine.

In general, rhetorical devices fall into three categories: phonological rhetorical devices, semantic rhetorical devices and syntactical rhetorical devices. Sometimes you can find other terms for these three categories, like phonetic devices, lexical devices, and syntactic devices.

They are essentially the same, all showing that these classifications are made in terms of sounds, words and sentences.

Phonological rhetorical devices make use of the phonological features of words. Some commonly-used phonological rhetorical devices are alliteration, consonance, assonance, onomatopoeia, etc.

Semantic rhetorical devices rely on the semantic associations and linguistic alterations. Some commonly used semantic rhetorical devices include simile, metaphor, transferred epithet, metonymy, synecdoche, personification, allusion, irony, oxymoron, hyperbole, understatement, euphemism, contrast, pun, syllepsis, zeugma, parody, paradox, etc.

Syntactical rhetorical devices are based on the balance of sentence structures or the emphasis on the key information, like repetition, catchword repetition, chiasmus, parallelism, antithesis, rhetoric question, anticlimax, etc.

 ## 5.2　Alliteration, Assonance, and Consonance

Lead-in Questions:

1. What is alliteration? Can we list some examples?

2. What is assonance? Can we list some examples?

3. What is consonance? Can we list some examples?

4. How can we use the above rhetorical devices to empower our language?

This section introduces three phonological rhetorical devices: alliteration, consonance and assonance. As their names suggest, they make use of the sound features of words, i.e. devices at the sound level. These three devices share one thing in common—the repetition of sound, but different types of sound repetition.

5.2.1 Alliteration

Alliteration is a very common rhetorical device that involves using words that begin with the same consonant sound. Or you can also understand it this way: Alliteration happens at the beginnings of a series of words; it is about the repetition of sound; the repeated sound is about consonant sounds, not vowels. For example, in "Peter Piper picked a peck of pickled peppers", all the words start with the /p/ sound. The repetition of /p/ at the beginnings of these words makes alliteration. This kind of repetition is usually used in oral English to practice pronunciation. In addition, alliteration is also used to achieve musical effect in language. Language learners often confuse the sounds with the letters. The repetition is not about the

same letter, but the same sound.

Let's look at the following examples, and judge whether there is alliteration in them.

e.g. 1. The wild winds whisk to the west.

e.g. 2. He felt a physical pain.

e.g. 3. Erin cooked cupcakes in the kitchen.

In Example 1, we can find "w" in "wild" "wind" and "west", and "wh" in "whisk". Both "w" and "wh" are pronounced as /w/ which is the repeated consonance. Therefore, it's easy to identify the alliteration in this sentence.

In Example 2, both "physical and "pain" start with the letter "p", but "p" in "physical" is combined with "h" to be pronounced as /f/. According to the definition, alliteration involves repetition of an initial sound, not the same letter, so "physical" and "pain" do not make alliteration. However, "felt" and "physical", despite the different letters, are used alliteratively because they have the same initial sound /f/.

In Example 3, "cook" and "cupcake" make alliteration with the same initial sound /k/, and in both words, the letter "c" is pronounced as /k/. Besides, "k" in "kitchen" is also pronounced as /k/, so these three words have the same initial consonant sound and make alliteration.

Alliteration is often used in poetry and other genres. The following example is from William Shakespeare's *Romeo and Juliet*:

e.g. 4. From forth the fatal loins of these two foes;
A pair of star-cross'd lovers take their life.

Example 4 shows alliteration with the repetition of /f/ in "forth" "fatal", and "foes", and repetition of /l/ in "loins" "lovers", and "life".

As a rhetorical device, alliteration is good for sound rhyme, musical effect, and significant emphasis, making the words attractive and appealing and easier to learn by readers. *Pride and Prejudice* and *Sense and Sensibility* are books that capture readers' attention. Idioms like "safe and sound" and "part and parcel" are easy to remember. Alliteration is also used in brand names, such as "Mickey Mouse" "Dunkin' Donuts" "Best Buy" "Coca-Cola", and so on.

Furthermore, alliteration adds flow and beauty to language. Read the following examples loud, and try to uncover any alliteration in them.

e.g. 5. Somewhere at this very moment a child is being born in America. Let it be our cause to give that child a happy home, a healthy family, and a hopeful future.

e.g. 6. This generation of soldiers, sailors, airmen, Marines, and Coast Guardsmen have volunteered in the time of certain danger. They are part of the finest fighting force that the world has ever known. They have served tour after tour of duty in distant, different, and difficult places.

5.2.2 Assonance

Another sound device is assonance. It is the repetition of vowel sounds in the stressed syllables of a sequence of words.

The English language has five vowels: "a" "e" "i" "o", and "u". When these vowels appear in different words, they are pronounced as different vowel sounds, and these vowel sounds are classified into short vowel sounds, long vowel sounds, and double vowel sounds. For example, in "Men sell the wedding bells", the short vowel sound /e/ is repeated in words "men" "sell" "wedding", and "bell". The repetition of /e/ in these words makes assonance.

Another example is assonance in the poem "Fire and Ice" by Robert Frost:

e.g. 7. Some say the world will end in fire,

　　　Some say in ice.

　　　From what I've tasted of desire

　　　I hold with those who favor fire.

　　　But if it had to perish twice,

　　　I think I know enough of hate

　　　To say that for destruction ice

　　　Is also great

　　　And would suffice.

In this poem, the vowel sound /aɪ/ is repeated in words "fire" "ice" "desire" "fire" "twice", and "suffice". This repetition makes assonance, and helps to create the beauty in sound.

Assonance is all about vowel sounds. Just like alliteration, assonance is often used as a tool to enhance the musical effect of the language and the pleasure of reading a literary work.

5.2.3 Consonance

Consonance refers to the repetition of the same sound in quick succession produced by consonants within a sentence or phrase. Opposite to assonance, consonance is the repetition of consonants, not the vowels. The repetitive sound is often found in the middle or at the end of a word. To put it simple, consonance is the repetition of internal or ending consonant sounds.

Here are some examples of consonance. Read them and try to identify the pleasing rhyme

created by consonance.

e.g. 8. The uncertain rustle of noi<u>se</u> cau<u>se</u>d my poi<u>se</u>.

e.g. 9. We are boun<u>d</u> by a bon<u>d</u> that can transcen<u>d</u> the beyon<u>d</u>.

e.g. 10. He stru<u>ck</u> a strea<u>k</u> of bad lu<u>ck</u>.

e.g. 11. He stoo<u>d</u> on the roa<u>d</u> and cri<u>ed</u>.

In a summary, alliteration is about the initial consonant sounds, consonance is about the middle and ending consonant sounds, and assonance is all about vowel sounds.

Simile

Lead-in Questions:

1. What is simile? Can we list some examples?

2. How can we use simile to empower our language?

"Life is like a box of chocolates; you never know what you're going to get" is a famous line from the movie *Forrest Gump*. Gump's mother compares life to a box of chocolates. Mom uses this special way to express her idea so that her words might be understood better by her son. What Mom tells Gump is a profound idea, which suggests that life is a mysterious journey and one can always be ready for surprises, be it good or bad, because life is uncertain—you don't ever know what's going to happen until it actually happens. This special way Mom uses is one of the most commonly used figures of speech—simile. Figures of speech are rhetorical devices in which words are made to mean differently from their literal meaning. Simile refers to a figure of speech that makes a comparison, showing similarities between two different things. Look at the following two sentences and decide which sentence features simile.

e.g. 12. Peter is as tall as his father.

e.g. 13. Peter is as tall as a tree.

According to its definition, a simile is a comparison between two different things which fall into different categories. Simile is not used in Example 12, as it is a comparative sentence. It is used in Example 13, because Peter and the tree are two different things.

A simile consists of three parts: tenor, vehicle and indicator of resemblance. For example, in "Life is like a box of chocolates", "life" is the tenor, "a box of chocolates" is the vehicle, and "like" is the indicator of resemblance. The primary function of simile is to help writers to make more emphatic and vivid descriptions. For example, when hearing remarks like "you are as slow as a snail", you immediately understand that you walk or do something so slowly that your friend might be upset with you. Snails are always associated with slow pace, and your slow pace is compared to that of a snail. The use of simile makes the language impressive and vivid. Other examples are "It's a hard day, and I've been working like a dog" "He smokes like a chimney", etc.

Simile is also used to attract people's attention and appeals directly to the senses of readers, encouraging their imagination to understand what is being communicated. Take simile used in advertisement as an example. "Seely" is a brand name for a mattress. The slogan for the mattress is "Sleeping on a Seely is like sleeping on a cloud". When "Seely" is compared to "cloud", the customers can imagine how soft, comfortable and cozy the mattress is. Simile makes the advertisement more persuasive and appealing.

In English, simile is also used in idioms or proverbs, for example, "He is as cunning as a fox". Complete the following idioms with words of animals.

1. as brave as _____
2. as funny as _____
3. as blind as _____
4. as wise as _____
5. as gentle as _____
6. to drink like _____
7. to eat (impolitely) like _____
8. to eat (a lot) like _____
9. to eat (a little) like _____
10. to fight like _____
11. to work like _____

The following are suggested answers.

1. lions
2. a monkey
3. a bat
4. an owl
5. a lamb
6. a fish
7. a pig
8. a horse

9. a bird

10. cats and dogs

11. a dog

More significantly, simile is often used in poetry and other literary works. Here is an example:

e.g. 14. O my Luve is like a red, red rose

That's newly sprung in June;

O my Luve is like the melody

That's sweetly played in tune.

These are the lines from the famous poem by Robert Burns who depicts the beauty of his beloved girl. These lines contain two similes which present the readers with an amazing picture of a young girl as beautiful as a red rose and as sweet as a piece of music.

Let's look at another example:

e.g. 15. Moments before sleep are when she feels most alive, leaping across fragments of the day, bringing each moment into the bed with her like a child with schoolbooks and pencils.

In Example 15, the readers are inspired to relate the writer's feelings to their personal experiences. Therefore, the use of similes makes it easier for the readers to understand what the writer expresses in a literary text. Otherwise, it would be too difficult to understand.

To sum up, similes allow the writers to express their ideas clearly and vividly. By creating some mental pictures or vivid images, writers make it easier to attract the readers' attention and appeal directly to their senses, and thus get their ideas across more effectively.

Words "like" and "as" are common indicators of resemblance. There are several other patterns. In "as… as" pattern, the first "as" is sometimes omitted. For example:

e.g. 16. His skin was (as) cold as ice.

Words such as "than" "as if" "as though" "seem" "resemble" "compare… to" "similar to" and "be likened to" are also used as indicators of resemblance.

 Metaphor

Lead-in Questions:

1. What are metaphors? Can we list some examples?

2. How can we use metaphors to empower our language?

e.g. 17. All the world's a stage,

And all the men and women merely players,

They have their exits and their entrances.

These lines are quoted from William Shakespeare's *As You Like It*. He compares the world to a stage and life to a play. When Shakespeare made the comparison, he employed a figure of speech—metaphor. A metaphor makes implied or hidden comparison between two totally different things, which have some characteristics in common. For example, a metaphor is used in "He is an early bird". "He" is definitely not a bird. However, a comparison is made to describe an association between an early bird and "He". As the idiom says "The early bird catches the worm", the person and the early bird share some common characteristics, i.e. doing something earlier.

Just like a simile which makes a comparison between two different things, a metaphor also makes a comparison, but indicators of resemblance are omitted in the metaphor. In other words, you can find tenor and vehicle in a metaphor, but can't find indicators like "like" "as", etc.

Look at again the example "He is an early bird". In this metaphor, "He" is the tenor, and "an early bird" is the vehicle. If both the tenor and vehicle are present in a metaphor, it is called a visible metaphor. If either the tenor or the vehicle is absent, it is called an invisible metaphor.

Let's look at the following example:

e.g. 18. Mary had butterflies in her stomach.

A metaphor can be easily identified in this sentence. Obviously, there was no butterfly in Mary's stomach, but she felt so nervous as if there had been butterflies flipping wings in her stomach.

A metaphor is undeniably a rhetorical device commonly used in poetry. Can you find out three metaphors in the first three lines of the following poem?

e.g. 19. The wind was a torrent of darkness among the gusty trees,

The moon was a ghostly galleon tossed upon cloudy seas,

The road was a ribbon of moonlight over the purple moor,

And the highwayman came riding—
Riding—riding—
The highwayman came riding, up to the old inn-door.

The first metaphor compares the wind to "a torrent of darkness". "Torrent" is a lot of water rushing or flowing violently. The second metaphor compares the moon to "a ghostly galleon". A galleon is a big old ship, the kind that would have carried Spanish gold across the seas. In this line, the moon is compared to a ship sailing through the sky. The third metaphor is about the road which is compared to "a ribbon of moonlight".

In this poem, the author uses metaphors to create a horrifying nighttime scene, a good setting for a sad, scary story. When the readers read the lines, they will naturally use their imagination to visualize the scene. The descriptions appeal directly to their senses. What's more, metaphors can add poetic flavor to language, which is like adding spice to food, making the language vivid and impressive.

Many students assume that it won't be difficult to identify a metaphor. In fact, there are various forms of metaphors, making it challenging to be recognized.

The simplest form of metaphors is the comparison between nouns. For example:

e.g. 20. America is a melting pot.

Readers can immediately identify the metaphor: America is compared to "a melting pot", and the similarity lies in the mixing. America is a place where different peoples, styles and cultures are mixed together. This is the simplest form of metaphors, but still there are some complicated forms. For example:

e.g. 21. A pattern with "of":
A policeman waved me out of the snake of traffic.

e.g. 22. An invisible metaphor:
The row of penguins at the dinner table nodded approval as he sat down.

In Example 21, the traffic is compared to the shape of a snake. In Example 22, the tenor is missing, with only the vehicle "penguins". The word "penguins" is used to refer to the guests who dressed up in suits and behaved in a way like penguins.

Here is one more example:

e.g. 23. Some books are to be tasted, others to be swallowed, and some few to be chewed and digested.

In Example 23, "books" is the tenor compared to "food", a vehicle which is absent in this sentence. It is an invisible metaphor. Verbs like "tasted" "swallowed" "chewed" and "digested" are closely related to something we eat, and they help to make the metaphor.

Look at the following examples, and identify the metaphors in them.

e.g. 24. The committee shot her ideas down one by one.

e.g. 25. The new movie was very popular. People flocked to see it.

e.g. 26. A heavy silence blanketed the room.

In Example 24, the committee's refusal is compared to a gun. In Example 25, people are compared to a herd of animals. In Example 26, silence is compared to a blanket.

 Exercise

Read the following questions and choose the correct answers.

1. The three appeals are the following **EXCEPT** _____.

    A. ethos   B. logos   C. pathos   D. egos

2. Which phonological device(s) is/are used in the following poem?

    A. Alliteration.   B. Consonance.

    C. Alliteration & Consonance.   D. Assonance.

The Eagle

Alfred, Lord Tennyson (1809–1892)

He clasps the crag with crooked hands;

Close to the sun in lonely lands,

Ringed with the azure world, he stands.

The wrinkled sea beneath him crawls;

He watches from his mountain walls,

And like a thunderbolt he falls.

3. A simile can be found in the following sentences **EXCEPT** _____.

    A. Living without an aim is like sailing without a compass

    B. He has a heart of stone and will of iron

    C. A crowd of people were around him, touching his body, feeling his legs, and bidding for him as if he had been a horse

D. He is only as short as a 10-year-old boy

4. A metaphor can be found in the following sentences **EXCEPT** _____.

A. Kisses are the flowers of love in bloom

B. His relation with his wife has not been fortunate

C. He pleaded for her forgiveness but Janet's heart was cold iron

D. Let your eyes drink up that milkshake sky

Unit 6
Rhetoric (II)

In this unit, more rhetorical devices and their expressive power will be discussed. Metonymy, synecdoche, paradox and oxymoron are also called figures of speech, which mean that words are made to mean differently from their literal meaning. Parallelism, antithesis and chiasmus involve variation in sentence structures for rhetorical effect, and they are usually labeled with syntactic devices. A knowledge of these rhetorical devices will help us become not only effective readers but also successful writers.

 Metonymy and Synecdoche　

Lead-in Questions:

1. What is metonymy? Can we list some examples?

2. What is synecdoche? Can we list some examples?

3. How can we use the above rhetorical devices to empower our language?

6.1.1 Metonymy

This section will explain two figures of speech—metonymy and synecdoche. They are so similar to each other that many students feel confused and cannot tell them apart. We may know this expression "lend me your ears". "Ears" does not refer to the organs on the head. It substitutes for "giving attention to others' words". This is the use of metonymy. Metonymy is a figure of speech that replaces the name of a thing with the name of something else, and these two things are closely associated with each other. We can also understand it this way: A is replaced by B, and B has some associations with A; whenever B is mentioned, it always reminds people of A.

One well-known example of metonymy is the saying, "The pen is mightier than the sword." This sentence has two examples of metonymy: (1) The "pen" does not mean the physical object we write with; it substitutes for "the written words", and "the written words" are associated with the "pen"; (2) The "sword" doesn't mean the weapon we use for violence; it substitutes for "military force", and "military force" is associated with "sword".

Look at the following examples, and find out metonymy in them.

e.g. 1. Let me give you a hand.

(hand = help)

e.g. 2. The White House will be announcing the decision around noon today.

(The White House = the President or others who work in the White House)

e.g. 3. Empty pockets never held anyone back. Only empty heads and empty hearts can do that.

(Empty pockets = poverty)

(empty heads = ignorance/dullness)

(empty hearts = unkindness/coldness)

One of the main purposes of using metonymy is to add flavor to the language, and it helps writers to express their contents in a poetic or unique way, drawing the readers' attention to what otherwise would not be noticed. Sometimes metonymy is also helpful to make statements concise. For instance, "*The Times* hasn't arrived at the press conference yet" is more concise than "The reporter from *The Times* hasn't arrived at the press conference yet".

Metonymy can be derived from the following sources:

(1) Body parts as names for the sense, behavior or ability:

e.g. 4. Friends, Romans, countrymen, lend me your ears.

(ears = attention)

(2) Names of people as names for their works or styles:

e.g. 5. He is studying Hemingway.

(Hemingway = Hemingway's novels or style)

(3) Names of clear signs of objects or people as names for the objects or those people:

e.g. 6. We must wait to hear from the crown until we make any further decisions.

(crown = king)

(4) Names of places as names for things produced there or for events that happened in those places:

e.g. 7. Watergate changed American politics.

(Watergate = the political scandal that happened in Watergate)

(5) Instruments or containers as names for the methods, positions or substances:

e.g. 8. The kettle is boiling.

(kettle = water in the kettle)

e.g. 9. The library has been very helpful to the students this morning.

(library = librarian)

(6) Trademarks or brands as names for the products:

e.g. 10. He was driving a Ford.

(Ford = Ford car)

(7) Locations as names for the governments, institutions or enterprises:

e.g. 11. Wall Street is in a panic.

(Wall Street = the financial institutions in the Wall Street)

6.1.2 Synecdoche

Some students find it difficult to distinguish metonymy from synecdoche. These two figures of speech resemble each other. Metonymy involves the substitution of the name of one thing for that of another. Synecdoche occurs when the name of a part is used to refer to the whole or vice versa. In other words, a part of something is used to refer to the whole entity, or a whole entity is used to refer to a part of something.

Let's look at the following examples:

e.g. 12. There are hungry mouths to feed.

The word "mouths" stands for people. When a part is used to substitute the whole, synecdoche is used.

e.g. 13. The poor creature could no longer endure her sufferings.

The word "creature" refers to an individual, not human beings in general. It is a substitution of the whole for a part; thus synecdoche is used.

Let's look at more examples about synecdoche.

e.g. 14. I've got a new set of wheels.

(wheels = cars, motorcycles, etc.)

e.g. 15. She wore gold around her neck.

(gold = chain)

e.g. 16. Two coffees, pleases.

(coffees = two cups of coffee)

e.g. 17. We need a couple of strong bodies for our team.

(bodies = people)

Metonymy is different from synecdoche in that in metonymy the word we employ is linked to the concept we are talking about, but it isn't actually a part. Let's compare the following two sentences:

e.g. 18. Her heart ruled her head.

e.g. 19. We had dinner at ten dollars a head.

Example 18 means that she acts according to her emotions rather than to her reasoning; "heart" refers to emotions, and "head" means reasoning. Therefore, metonymy is used in Example 18. In Example 19, the word "head" refers to a person, and "head" is also a part of a person. Therefore, synecdoche is used in Example 19.

Paradox and Oxymoron

Lead-in Questions:

1. What is paradox? Can we list some examples?

2. What is oxymoron? Can we list some examples?

3. How can we use the above rhetorical devices to empower our language?

6.2.1 Paradox

In Shakespeare's *Hamlet*, when the hero states "I must be cruel to be kind", we may feel very surprised. In our common sense, it is unkind to be cruel to someone. On the surface, this statement does not seem to make much sense. These two words "cruel" and "kind" are contradictory to each other. How can an individual conduct kindness while doing evil? Hamlet is talking about his mother. He intends to kill Claudius who killed his father and married his mother. His attempt to kill his step-father will be a tragedy for his mother. However, he does not want his mother to be the lover of his father's murderer any longer, so he believes killing his step-father will be for her own good. On a second thought, the contradiction makes sense and reveals unexpected insights. This is an example of paradox.

In this section, two rhetorical devices will be introduced— paradox and oxymoron. They have something in common—contradiction. The contradiction can be found at different levels. We may be wondering why writers make their words confusing and difficult to understand. Reading is like a game. Readers enjoy more when they figure out the hidden meanings out of the writing. Therefore, paradox can give readers more pleasure.

The term "paradox" is from the Greek word "paradoxon" that means being contrary to expectations, existing belief or perceived opinion. It is the juxtaposition of a set of seemingly contradictory concepts that reveal a hidden and/or unexpected truth.

Look at the following examples:

e.g. 20. No news is good news.

e.g. 21. I know one thing: that I know nothing.

e.g. 22. Cheapest is the dearest.

e.g. 23. Whatever you do will be insignificant, but it is very important that you do it.

e.g. 24. More haste, less speed.

e.g. 25. I can resist anything but temptation.

All of them sound quite absurd and illogical. But when we read them again, we see some truth, unexpected and interesting. The seemingly absurd and illogical statements can impress the readers and convey some thought-provoking ideas. Take "a child is the father of a man" as an example. Is it nonsense? How can a child be the father of a man? On the surface, this statement has seemingly incorrect proposition, for only a man can be the father of a child. However, when we explore deep into its meaning, we see the truth. It is a fact that the childhood experiences become the basis for all adult behavior. The childhood of a person shapes his life and consequently a child becomes the "father" of an adult. The point is conveyed in an implicit way. It is the same as "failure is the mother of success". In this sense, reading involves more thinking.

In poetry, paradox is sometimes used to convey a tone of irony to its readers. For example:

e.g. 26. It is a paradox that computers need maintenance so often, since they are meant to save people's time.

e.g. 27. As an actor, he's a paradox—he loves being in the public eye but also deeply values and protects his privacy.

e.g. 28. All animals are equal, but some are more equal than others.

To sum up, a paradox may be hard or even impossible to believe; yet the contradiction can make sense if the readers read between the lines.

6.2.2 Oxymoron

An oxymoron is a phrase that seems to contain contradictory elements. It is essentially a two-word paradox or a condensed paradox at the phrase level. Contradiction is a paradox at the sentence level and oxymoron is at the word level. Oxymoron binds together two contradictory words with contrary or contradictory meanings, such as a living death, a deafening silence, pain for pleasure, unpopular celebrity, victorious defeat, adult children, valuable rubbish, fearful bravery, a wonderful lousy poem, true lie, bitter-sweet memory, make haste slowly, etc.

Oxymoron is used for creating some sort of dramatic effect, and they may also be used to make people think. Such phrases as "a wonderful lousy poem" and "a bitter-sweet memory" indicate that an object or a matter can have two different qualities at once, making it a subject for study and analysis.

In brief, the difference between a paradox and an oxymoron lies in the fact that a paradox may consist of a sentence or even a group of sentences, while an oxymoron is a combination of two contradictory or opposite words. A paradox seems contradictory to the truth, but it does contain an implied truth. An oxymoron, however, may produce a dramatic effect, but it does not make as much sense as a paradox does.

 Parallelism and Antithesis

Lead-in Questions:

1. What is parallelism? Can we list some examples?

2. What is antithesis? Can we list some examples?

3. How can we use the above rhetorical devices to empower our language?

In this section, two more rhetorical devices, parallelism and antithesis, will be discussed respectively.

6.3.1 Parallelism

Speaking of parallelism, we may think of the famous quote "I came, I saw, I conquered". This famous remark is made by Julius Caesar, the Roman general and statesman. In this quote, each clause begins with "I" plus a verb. The repetition of this grammatical structure makes parallelism, and the language is forceful, presenting readers with an invincible image in ancient Rome.

Parallelism is a rhetorical device in which words or sentence structures are repeated deliberately for effect. Repetition of a set of grammatical structures shows that a pair or a list of ideas have equal weight or share equal importance. For example:

e.g. 29. We have seen the state of our Union in the endurance of rescuers, working past exhaustion. We've seen the unfurling of flags, the lighting of candles, the giving of blood, the saying of prayers—in English, Hebrew, and Arabic.

e.g. 30. Tell me and I forget. Teach me and I may remember. Involve me and I will learn.

6.3.2 Antithesis

Antithesis is a rhetorical device in which two opposite or contrasting ideas are put together in adjacent phrases, clauses, or sentences to achieve a contrasting effect. It emphasizes the idea of contrast by parallel structures to draw the attention of the readers. For example, "That's one small step for man, one giant leap for mankind" was proclaimed by Neil Armstrong, the first person to walk on the moon. In this famous quote, "small step" and "giant leap" are contrasting ideas, and they are presented in parallel structures. With the use of antithesis, this quote highlights the significance of the moon-landing.

Antithesis can empower the language with magic. First of all, since antithesis emphasizes the contrast between two ideas, the structure of the phrases/clauses is usually similar. As a result, readers' attention can be captured instantly. Secondly, it conveys meaning more vividly than ordinary words do. When contrasting ideas are brought together, they are expressed more emphatically. It is this balance and emphasis that help make the point of the writer memorable. Most importantly, antithesis presents the readers with aesthetic art of simplicity, symmetry and precision. That's why people all over the world always associate Neil Armstrong with his famous words, and antithesis produces the magic that makes his words extraordinary and unforgettable.

It is not difficult to identify antithesis, as opposite words can always be found, like "small step" and "giant leap". Actually, antithesis is not only about opposite words, but two opposite or contrasting ideas.

Look at the following examples:

e.g. 31. We observe today not a victory of party but a celebration of freedom.

e.g. 32. Out of sight, out of mind.

Opposites can't be found in the above examples, but each example produces contrasting ideas. Generally speaking, opposites can often, not always, be found in antithesis, and contrasting ideas are also effective.

Here are more examples:

e.g. 33. I have a dream that my four little children will one day live in a nation where they will not be judged by the color of their skin but by the content of their character. I have a dream today!

e.g. 34. Integrity without knowledge is weak and useless, and knowledge without integrity is dangerous and dreadful.

e.g. 35. The world will little note, nor long remember what we say here, but it can never forget what they did here.

Chiasmus

Lead-in Questions:

1. What is chiasmus? Can we list any examples?

2. How can we use chiasmus to empower our language?

Chiasmus is a rhetorical device in which the second half of an expression is balanced against the first, with the parts reversed.

e.g. 36. One should eat to live, not live to eat.

In this sentence, we can find a pattern like "eat to live" and "live to eat".

Chiasmus is a Greek term meaning "diagonal arrangement". It is used to describe two successive clauses or sentences where the keywords or phrases are repeated in both clauses, but in reverse order. As its name suggests, chiasmus is sometimes known as a crisscross rhetorical device. In its strict classical sense, however, chiasmus refers to reverse grammatical structure or ideas of sentences given that the same words and phrases are not repeated. For example, "We ran away quickly; speedily, we fled." Now the term "chiasmus" applies broadly to almost all "crisscross" structures, which has become a commonly accepted concept these days.

There is a general pattern for chiasmus: ABBA. When the first clause contains two words A and B, the second clause contains the same words, but in reverse order.

[Clause 1] ... A... B..., [Clause 2] ... B... A...

In this pattern, "A" or "B" can be either a single word, or a group of words.

Read the following examples and identify the reversed pairs in each sentence:

e.g. 37. Mankind must put an end to war, or war will put an end to mankind.

e.g. 38. Let us never negotiate out of fear. But let us never fear to negotiate.

e.g. 39. We don't mistrust each other because we're armed; we're armed because we mistrust each other.

e.g. 40. A statesman is a politician who places himself at the service of the nation. A politician is a statesman who places the nation at his service.

With its unique structural symmetry, chiasmus, like a mirror, shines in writing and speaking. It is public speakers' favorite technique, making their speech impressive and interesting, humorous and witty.

Since chiasmus has symmetrical structure, it won't be difficult for readers to expect the latter part. Complete the following blanks.

1. You forget what you want to remember,
and _____.

2. They don't care about how much you know until _____.

3. My job is not to represent Washington to you, but _____.

4. Do I love you because you're beautiful? Or _____?

The following are the suggested answers.

1. you remember what you want to forget

2. they know how much you care

3. to represent you to Washington

4. are you beautiful because I love you

To sum up, chiasmus reverses grammatical structure in phrases or clauses, and it expresses complex ideas musically, wittily, and memorably.

 Exercise

Read the following questions and choose the correct answers.

1. Which of the following is not a semantic rhetorical device?

    A. Metaphor.   B. Parallelism.   C. Metonymy.   D. Simile.

2. Simile can be found in the following sentences **EXCEPT** _____.

    A. Her face resembled a red apple

    B. Shakespeare compared the world to a stage

    C. There are a lot of good heads in our university

    D. He treats his child as the apple in the eye

3. In which sentence is synecdoche used?

    A. The buses in America are on strike now.

    B. The fox goes very well with your cap.

    C. Brain is mightier than muscle.

    D. I had the muscle and they made money out of it.

4. Paradox can be found in the following sentences **EXCEPT** _____.

    A. I'm not young enough to know everything

    B. He is as welcome as a storm

    C. Those who have eyes apparently see little

    D. If we want peace, be prepared for a war

5. In which sentence is antithesis used?

    A. Love is an ideal thing, marriage a real thing.

    B. Do I love you because you're beautiful? Or are you beautiful because I love you?

    C. This is not only just what I wanted, but also just what I needed.

    D. The problem was not in planning or in development, but rather in production.

6. In which sentence is metonymy used?

    A. Let me give you a hand.

    B. There are about 100 hands working in his factory.

    C. We need a couple of strong bodies for our team.

    D. We've got some new blood in the organization.

7. Oxymoron can be found in the following sentences **EXCEPT** _____.

    A. Love is a sweet torment

    B. The fans called the game a victorious defeat

    C. No light, but rather darkness visible

    D. An ambassador is an honest man who lies abroad for the good of his country

8. Parallelism can be found in the following speeches **EXCEPT** _____.

    A. Our transportation crisis will be solved by a bigger plane or a wider road, mental illness with a pill, poverty with a law, slums with a bulldozer, urban conflict with a gas, racism with a goodwill gesture.

    B. But at the end of the day, we can have the most dedicated teachers, the most supportive parents, the best schools in the world—and none of it will make a difference, none of it will matter unless all of you fulfill your responsibilities, unless you show up to those schools, unless you pay attention to those teachers, unless you listen to your parents and grandparents and other adults and put in the hard work it takes to succeed.

    C. You want to be a doctor, or a teacher, or a police officer? You want to be a nurse or an architect, a lawyer or a member of our military? You're going to need a good education for every single one of those careers. You cannot drop out of school and just drop into a good job. You've got to train for it and work for it and learn for it.

    D. My message to all of you today is this: Do not waste a minute living someone else's dream. It takes a lot of real work to discover what brings you joy.

Unit 7
Critical Thinking (I)

The fact that we live in an information age doesn't mean that everyone in it is capable of integrating the information for one's own use. Actually, one may get lost in the sea of information if he/she lacks proper judgment.

Our age advocates innovation out of curiosity, imagination, and critical thinking. Critical thinking triggers more frequent reflection, more effective team work and more optimized decision making. The core competitiveness of innovative talents is exactly the ability of critical thinking, which is the key to success and happiness rather than an abstract concept far away from our daily life.

So, what is critical thinking? Are there any rules we can follow in the thinking process? This unit will unveil the attributes of mysterious critical thinking and provide us with practical tools for case analysis.

 Critical Thinking: The 3Cs Framework

Lead-in Questions:

1. What is critical thinking?

2. What does the 3Cs framework of critical thinking refer to?

Now, take a look at this.

$$A\ B\ C$$

What can you see?

"A, B, C", right? It is quite obvious. However, could it also be "A, 13, C"? We may say as this is an English textbook, we don't link it to a number. Actually, that is not the point. It is all because of our conventional thinking. We are often shaped by the so-called common sense, so we fail to have different angles. How can we step out of our conventional thinking to view the world critically? In this unit, we are going to focus on critical thinking.

When others think of something as true, you claim it to be false. When others think of something as good, you claim it to be bad. When others think of something as beautiful, you claim it to be ugly. Are those responses assumed to be critical thinking? Does critical thinking refer to the utter denial of others and being totally different in viewpoint? The answer is definitely no. Critical thinking doesn't mean fault-finding. It highlights one's own judgment instead of blind acceptance or objection. One is supposed to put forward one's own claim after meticulous certification in the spirit of challenge. In essence, critical thinking is a mode of thinking, where judgment or conclusion is formed on the basis of objective analysis or evaluation on certain questions or phenomena. Three steps are involved in the process of critical thinking: to question, to judge on the basis of facts and logic, to express the conclusion clearly. Only by following these steps can one's critical thinking develop from a certain kind of awareness to an attitude, then an ability and finally a habit.

The concept of critical thinking still sounds a little abstract; how about taking a coin as an example. When we mention "a coin", what occurs to us first? Maybe it is the saying: "Every coin has two sides." This is one of the most popular sayings among students and too widely-used in their composition writing. Do you agree with this statement?

Now, let's begin the journey of critical thinking.

Step 1: Challenging

Have you ever doubted the truth of the above-mentioned saying? Does every coin really have only two sides?

Step 2: Certifying

Let's have a closer look. Every coin has one, two, three sides at least: the head, the tail and the side in between. Come on, no coin is flat; it is three dimensional.

A more careful look may help us approach the truth. Now, we enter into the third step.

Step 3: Claiming

Every coin has three sides at least.

These are the 3Cs of critical thinking. Let's try to put them into use.

Here is a piece of news:

e.g. 1.   **China's Auto Sales Slow, but New Energy Cars Outshine**

China's auto sales expanded at the slowest pace this year in September as weak sales of commercial cars weigh on growth. Approximately 1.98 million cars were sold in China last month, a year-on-year rise of 2.5 percent, while output increased 4.2 percent to 2 million

units, the China Association of Automobile Manufacturers (CAAM) said in a report published Monday. In the first nine months, output and sales stood at 17.22 million and 17 million, respectively, up 8.1 percent and 7 percent respectively, but growth was significantly down from the rates seen during the same period last year. The CAAM attributed the slowdown to sluggish performances in commercial cars. Last month, sales of commercial cars totalled 287,600 units, down 16 percent from a year earlier. The CAAM made an earlier forecast that market demand for automobiles would hit 23.83 million units this year, representing a 8.3-percent rise from 2013. Bucking the broader trend, sales of new energy cars saw strong growth on the back of government support to the industry. In the first nine months, a total 38,163 new energy cars were sold in China, 2.8 times the volume seen during the same period last year, the CAAM said. China has rolled out a set of measures to promote the use of new energy vehicles in its bid to save energy and combat pollution, including tax exemptions, subsidies for car purchases and requirement for government organs to buy more new energy cars.

The title "China's Auto Sales Slow, but New Energy Cars Outshine" means that new energy cars sell much better than other types of automobiles. This is the title and also the conclusion based on the statistics from the news. When we spot such key information as sales of commercial cars "down 16 percent from a year earlier" and sales of new energy cars "2.8 times the volume seen during the same period last year", we may think we're going to have a much greener environment!

This is news full of figures. It seems to be reliable. As Mark Twain said: "Figures don't lie…" But is it true?

Step 1: Challenging

Are numbers reliable?

Please pay attention. In Example 1, "down 16 percent" still means over 200,000 units a month for the sale of commercial cars, yet "2.8 times for new energy cars" only means around 40,000 units a month. We cannot only pay attention to the percentages and times; we should know what the actual number is. In this case, there is still a long way for us to go to have a greener environment just by the use of new energy cars.

Step 2: Certifying

We live in the information age; we live with facts and numbers every day. We depend on them to make judgments and make decisions. But without certifying them, what we are going to make are only mistakes. By the way, the original sentence from Mark Twain is: "Figures don't lie; but liars figure." Numbers are sometimes misinterpreted, which can be misleading.

Step 3: Claiming

Based on the first two steps, we can now safely claim that numbers are not always reliable. Challenging, certifying, claiming, the 3Cs of critical thinking guide us to think critically. The new claim here is going to be the starting point for a new round of critical thinking. It is going to be challenged again. So, to challenge or not to challenge, that is the challenge.

 Common Logical Fallacies (I)

Lead-in Questions:

1. What do Hasty Generalization and Begging the Question / Circular Reasoning refer to?

2. How does Slippery Slope form?

3. What is the weakness of Bandwagon Fallacy?

Sometimes we do feel that the so-called fact or truth is a little subjective or ambiguous in a certain way; either it concerns the international situation or global economic development or it is simply related to interpersonal relationship or our personal life. We are eager to challenge it but do not know how to be to the point and identify the exact weakness. How to stand out from the quarreling crowds? What are the common logical fallacies underlying there? Next, we are going to screen them.

Plato, Galileo, Marx, Darwin and Freud, do you know they share something in common? They are all great giants in human history and there is one more thing they share—big beard. So can we say they are all great because they have big beard or their greatness must somehow be related to this fact? Do you agree with this argument? Of course not. There is something wrong with it, but what, exactly? There is no evidence showing how beards cause their greatness. A beard is not a guarantee of greatness. The conclusion doesn't follow the reasoning: The great thinkers have beards; therefore, their beards cause their greatness.

Here is another example:

e.g. 2. We do not know that Statement A is true.
　　　Therefore,
　　　Statement A is false.

Imagine, for instance, that A is the claim that life apart from earth exists, and someone argues that because we don't know that there is any such life, it does not exist. The premise is about our lack of knowledge.

Obviously, some of the arguments have weaknesses. In this section, we will look at several types of logical fallacies.

7.2.1 Hasty Generalization

Look at the following example:

e.g. 3. Mark is left-handed.

Mark is very creative.

Left-handed people are creative.

Here is the fallacy: An isolated example is used to stand for the general.

e.g. 4. Quite several women road killers are reported.

All women are bad drivers.

This is expanding some for all.

We either replace the whole by the part or use personal experience / an isolated example for the general; it is drawing conclusion too quickly. We call this Hasty Generalization.

7.2.2 Begging the Question / Circular Reasoning

Look at the following dialog:

e.g. 5. A: Why are you so fat?

B: Because I eat too much.

A: Why do you eat too much?

B: Because I am fat.

This is a typical case of begging the question or circular reasoning: The answer and the question itself are in circular.

Let's look at another example:

e.g. 6. Differences between the roles that males and females are expected to play are not fixed by our genetic make-up but are learned in each individual's social development. Thus, gender is something that is learned rather than something which has a biological cause.

The argument starts with the claim that gender roles are not biological in origin but are learned in social development. The conclusion just repeats the claim. The argument has not moved from a reason to a conclusion: The ending is exactly the beginning. Circular argument is weak in persuading us to accept the conclusion simply because there is no progress in the reasoning process at all.

7.2.3 Slippery Slope

The problem with circular arguments is that they don't go anywhere, yet the problem with slippery slope arguments is that they go too far too quickly.

The slippery slope is a set of interconnected reasons, each of which is necessary for the whole reasoning structure. The weakness of the argument is: If any of the steps is taken down, the slippery slope can be challenged; if it is challenged, then what follows is unconvincing.

Here is one example:

e.g. 7. A: If the oil price goes down,

the oil consumption is going to go up.

B: Oil resources are going to dry up,

and human being is going to go die soon.

7.2.4 Bandwagon Fallacy

Look at the following dialogs:

e.g. 8. A: Look! Everyone goes to the party in dress. You should do the same as well.

B: I should go in a dress.

e.g. 9. A: Many students in our class have their own mobile phones.

B: I should have one as well.

e.g. 10. A: Many people I know give their votes to Joe Biden.

B: He must be a competent president, so I vote for him.

That many people do something does not necessarily mean it is a wise choice. That many people believe something does not mean it is correct or trustworthy. This is only following the suite or copying others. This is Bandwagon Fallacy.

 Common Logical Fallacies (II)

Lead-in Questions:

1. What does Either-or Reasoning / Black or White refer to?

2. What does Red Herring / Irrelevant to the Central Issue refer to?

3. Can two wrongs be turned into one right? Why?

4. What is the relationship between chronology and causality?

5. What does the Latin phrase "Ad Hominem" mean?

7.3.1 Either-or Reasoning / Black or White

Look at the following dialog:

e.g. 11. A: Someone finished the exam early.

B: Either really smart or really stupid.

What is wrong here? The issue is reduced to only two alternatives: either black or white, true or false, ugly or beautiful. Actually, there are many possibilities between the two opposite sides.

7.3.2 Red Herring / Irrelevant to the Central Issue

Look at the following dialog:

e.g. 12. A: The syrup tastes sweet.

B: The syrup will cure your fever.

What A says is about "the taste", while what B says is about "the function" of the medicine. Their points are irrelevant.

e.g. 13. A: Natural catastrophes such as earthquakes are beyond human control.

B: Human beings have no freedom of choice concerning their action.

Statement A is about "natural events", while Statement B is about "human's choices about their action".

When we are reasoning, try our best to build up the link between the evidence and the conclusion. If not, the real argument is ignored, while something that is irrelevant to the central issue is attacked instead. This is Red Herring: being irrelevant to the central issue.

7.3.3 Turning Two Wrongs into One Right

Look at another dialog:

e.g. 14. A: Why are you unhappy today?

B: It's not fair that I got into trouble for forgetting my textbooks.

A: Teachers always say that you should not forget your textbooks.

B: But lots of students in my class forget their textbooks. Lots of students do the same thing, so it is not fair to get me in trouble for this!

Though A appeals to a simple form of justice, it is unconvincing. Two wrongs simply cannot be turned into one right.

7.3.4 Post Hoc / After This, Therefore Because of This

Here is a typical example:

> e.g. 15. A: Why are you in uniform today?
>
> B: I am going to take a very important test.
>
> A: What?
>
> B: You know, before uniforms are introduced at our School, we ranked only 8 out of 20 district schools on a nationwide math test. But the following year, when we wear uniforms, we ranked No.1!
>
> A: Wow! Magic uniform!

Things happen one after another but not necessarily cause another. That one thing followed another may simply be a coincidence. Chronology does not equal causality.

7.3.5 Ad Hominem / Against the Man

Look at the following dialog:

> e.g. 16. A: We have a lot in common with chimpanzees because we have evolved from a common ancestor.
>
> B: You're close-minded and stupid. You don't know anything!

We should focus on the issue itself rather than attacking the opponent personally.

> e.g. 17. A: I failed in the final exam this time, because the new teacher doesn't teach well.

Let's try to analyze the reasons more objectively.

We have introduced several typical types of logical fallacies. Review Section 7.2 and Section 7.3 and then do some practice. Next time when we're going to challenge others, we can spot those fallacies and be quite to the point.

How to Certify (I): Evidence

Lead-in Questions:

1. What are the major types of evidence?

2. What does the ARTS rule of choosing evidence refer to?

Where can we get the evidence needed for our certification? Which are more convincing as certifying tools, personal experiences or statistics? We can never get strong by simply listing and piling the evidence. What we really need to know is how to search for evidence and then classify and evaluate it. We can get what we want if we know the ARTS rule.

Certifying, namely justifying the challenge, is the second step of the critical thinking framework. The basis for persuasiveness in certifying is surely the evidence. Now, let's look at different types of evidence and where we can get them.

7.4.1 Types of Evidence

1. Data

We can get data from observation, field study, interviews, questionnaires, surveys, libraries, Internet research, facts, quotes, statistics, graphics, etc.

But we have to know that data, when used as evidence, have limitations. For example, the data may be insufficient or non-typical; the way of getting the data and interpreting the data may be questionable. Data as evidence have both strengths and limitations.

2. Personal Experiences

The most direct evidence is our personal experiences, which can show our personal connection to the issue and arouse the readers' or listeners' interest and sympathy. Similarly, personal experiences as evidence have strong points and weak points. And the weak points are obvious: It might be insufficient and lead to hasty generalization; also, it might be unscientific and hard to prove.

3. Hypothetical Examples, Cases, and Scenarios

Personal experiences as evidence are the most direct ones. However, this doesn't mean we can only use something that truly happened as evidence. Hypothetical examples, cases, and scenarios can be used as well. We may wonder how something hypothetical, namely something assumed, something only existing in our thinking can be used as evidence. That's because they have strong imaginative appeal. And this feature is their limitation at the same time, because we will still doubt whether they are possible to happen or not. So, hypothetical examples, cases, and scenarios are persuasive only if they seem plausible.

7.4.2 Rule of Selecting Evidence

We can obtain abundant evidence if we collect the above-mentioned three types together. Here comes the next problem. When we get different kinds of data, personal experiences and hypothetical examples, cases, and scenarios at our hand, we may get lost about how to make a proper choice. Here comes the ARTS rule of choosing evidence: (1) **Accurate.** Remember, we are not supposed to overstate or understate the evidence. (2) **Relevant.** Only the evidence closely related to our argument can hold water. (3) **Typical.** Always select the typical and the usual evidence to make sense. (4) **Sufficient.** Our evidence needs to be adequate enough to be convincing.

Keep the types of evidence and the rule of selecting evidence in mind, and we will know where to go next time when we want to collect our evidence.

 Exercises

I. **Mark true (T) or false (F) for the following statements.**

   1. Critical thinking means objecting others when they claim something to be correct. ( )

   2. Never agree with anyone. This is exactly what critical thinking is about. ( )

   3. Critical thinking means never following others' ideas without any certifying. ( )

   4. The news based on data is always reliable. ( )

   5. Figures from statistics are objective and trustworthy. ( )

   6. Whenever we have doubt about any argument, we can directly put forward our own claim. ( )

   7. The information age enables us to make a ready judgment and decision. ( )

   8. Once a claim is made after certifying, it is unquestionable. ( )

   9. Critical thinking is a cycling process, in which the claim out of the first round turns out to be the starting point of a new round of reasoning. ( )

  10. Personal experiences cannot be used as evidence simply because they are personal. ( )

II. **Identify the logical fallacy in the following statements.**

   1. A majority of people disagree with this legislation; therefore it is a bad idea.

                                             ( )

   2. The two boys are handsome.

    Both of them come from Class Two.

    All the boys of Class Two are handsome.

                                             ( )

   3. Everyone is doing it this way, so the way must be correct.

                                             ( )

4. A: Why are you so busy?

   B: Because I work constantly

   A: Why do you work constantly?

   B: Because I am busy.

   ( )

5. A: I love autumn!

   B: You simply have no common sense. You know nothing at all.

   ( )

6. Each time I get my car washed on Wednesday recently; it rains. So I will never wash my car on Wednesday.

   ( )

7. A: He is good at drawing.

   B: He must be a competent monitor.

   ( )

8. A. The epidemic has caused a great loss in economy.

   B: The world economy is going to recess and human being will perish soon.

   ( )

9. A: You look unhappy today?

   B: It's not fair that I got into trouble for using mobile phone in class.

   A: Teachers always say that you should not play your mobile phone in class.

   B: But quite a few students in my class do so. Quite a few students do the same thing, so it is not fair to get me in trouble for this!

   ( )

10. We are going to negotiate with the company; we can either win or lose.

    ( )

Unit 8

Critical Thinking (II)

Do you want to visualize your thoughts with graphic illustration? Are you eager to indulge in the charm of reasoning? Are you willing to distinguish yourself in your study and work by innovative ideas and their unique representations? Do you want to achieve success by effective time management? What you need is a powerful helper—a mind map. What are the basic elements of a mind map? What are the common types and how to put them into proper use? Let's enter into the wonderland of mind maps.

 How to Certify (II): Mind Map

Lead-in Questions:

1. How can we summarize the major types and functions of mind maps?

2. What is the function of mind maps?

3. Can we design a mind map of any topic/idea by using one type of the mind maps mentioned in this section?

If we want to be powerful, we have to find evidence. Although we have already learned different types of evidence and the ARTS rule of finding them, we may still do not know how to organize them and make them work for us. A magic tool will be introduced to help us.

It is an excellent tool to map out our thoughts. It is a type of diagram used to visually display information in a relational way. Typically, it starts with a central idea (a word and/ or an image). It is a bit like a tree looked at from above, with its branches radiating out in all directions from the trunk. It is also the easiest way to put information into our brain and to take information out of our brain. It contains mere keywords, colors, spatial arrangement of branches, pictures, and symbols. It makes study, work, and thinking organized and enjoyable! It is a magic tool!

The above descriptions may remind us of pictures, maps, charts, lists, etc. A mind map, as a magic tool, is all in one. There are many ways for us to build the fit mind map. Here are five

major types of mind maps:

8.1.1 Circle Maps

Circle maps are tools used to help define a thing or an idea. It is our frame of reference or certain aspects about what we have already known. We list all the information we know about a thing or an idea so as to generate something new. In the center of the circle, we put a word, number, picture, sign or symbol to represent the object, person, or idea we are trying to focus on. In the outside circle, any relevant information is listed as the context (see Figure 8–1).

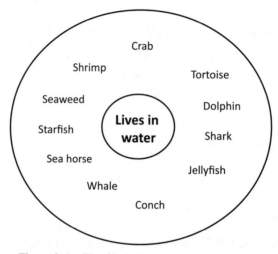

Figure 8–1　The Circle Map of "Lives in Water"

8.1.2 Bubble Maps

Bubble maps are used to describe qualities. Adjectives and adjective phrases are typical descriptive words. In the central circle, we write the word or the idea being described. In the surrounding circles, the adjectives or adjective phrases are listed to describe qualities (see Figure 8–2).

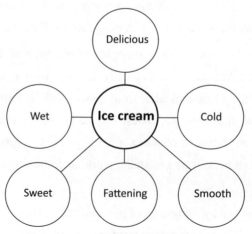

Figure 8–2　The Bubble Map of "Ice Cream"

8.1.3 Tree Maps

Tree maps are used to classify and group things. On the top line, write the category name. Below it, write sub-categories. Below each sub-category, write specific members of the group (see Figure 8–3). Surely, some things belong to multiple groups.

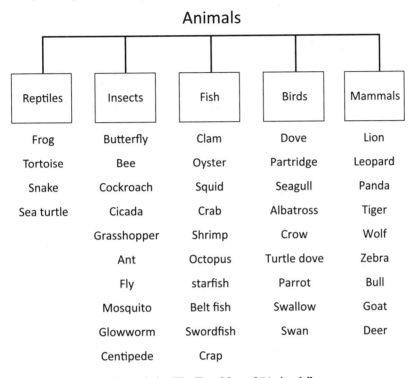

Figure 8–3　The Tree Map of "Animals"

8.1.4 Brace Maps

Brace maps help us understand the relationship between a whole physical object and its parts. It is useful in analyzing the structure of an item. On the line to the left, write the name of the whole object. On the lines within the first brace to the right, write the major parts of the object, and then follow within the next set of braces with the subparts of each major part (see Figure 8–4).

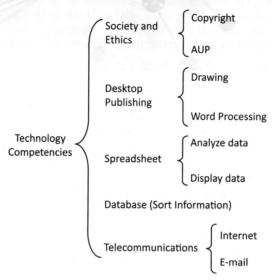

Figure 8–4　The Brace Map of "Technology Competencies"

8.1.5 Flow Maps

They are used to explain the order of events. In the outside rectangle, write the name of the event or sequence. The inside rectangles list the steps or events that follow from beginning to end (see Figure 8–5).

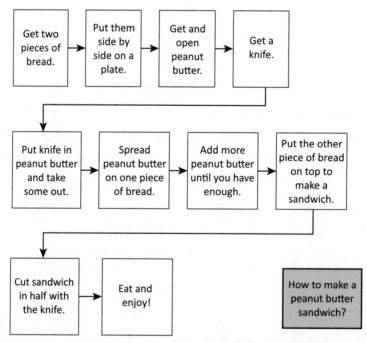

Figure 8–5　The Flow Map of "How to Make a Peanut Butter Sandwich"

Now, let's summarize: circle maps are for defining things or ideas; bubble maps are for describing qualities; tree maps are for classifying and grouping things; brace maps are for showing the relationship between the whole and the part; flow maps are for explaining the order of events.

Mind maps are practical tools, making our ideas clear, vivid, graphic, organized, and logical. Actually, drawing mind maps is a way of thinking. We can develop our own type of mind maps. The following is about when and where we can put mind maps into use.

First, as learners, we can use it for remembering, note taking, essay writing and presentation preparing as well. Then, as professionals, we can use it for planning, overviewing, organizing, problem analyzing, interviewing, communicating, negotiating, training, meetings and projects, etc. By using it, we can quickly identify and understand the structure of a subject and see the way that pieces of information fit together. It is very versatile to visualize, structure and organize almost any kind of information. It is a map of our mind.

 How to Claim: Logic (I)

Lead-in Questions:

1. What is a claim?

2. What is induction?

3. What is comparative argument?

4. What is causal argument?

Are you ready to claim? Does a claim mean that we put forward our own idea? Can we claim about anything? We claim about reality, truth, the way things are and values. Claims are our arguments. When we are trying to answer questions like: To what category does this thing belong? What are the causes or consequences of this phenomenon? To what is this similar? What is the worth or value of this thing? What action should we take?

We are claiming.

We live; we observe; we discover; we analyze; we judge; we claim.

We are reasoning every day. We are making arguments every day. When we present arguments in speaking or writing, we try to persuade others by giving reasons or citing evidence to back up our claims.

We highly rely on facts, because "Facts speak louder than words". But facts alone rarely convince. In order to make a persuasive argument, facts need to be related to one another in a logical manner. This is what we call as reasoning. Here are commonly accepted rules for it.

Induction is the process of reasoning from specific facts or occurrences to general

principles, theories, and rules. In inductive reasoning, individual cases or examples lead to a general conclusion. The assumption behind inductive reasoning is that known cases can provide us with information about unknown ones. Inductive reasoning is used both to generalize from observations and to identify the cause of a set of phenomena. Actually, we rely on induction constantly in everyday life. Let's look at the following example:

e.g. 1. A: Tom has been absent for class for the past three days.
　　　B: Today, he'll probably be absent again.

In this case, we base our prediction about what might happen on what we have already known.

8.2.1 Comparative Argument

Now, let's look at two different types of inductive reasoning. If one event, idea, or thing is compared with another to make a conclusion no matter whether they are similar enough to generalize or infer, this reasoning pattern is called comparative argument. Let's look at the following examples:

e.g. 2. A: Three of my friends wear long hair.
　　　B: So, I will follow.

e.g. 3. A: Whenever there is a holiday, the department stores have sales.
　　　B: This Children's Day, they will probably have sales.

8.2.2 Causal Argument

If we believe that one thing is the reason (cause) that another thing happens (effect), we may want to either reproduce that relationship to cause that effect again, or prevent the relationship from happening again. This pattern of reasoning is called causal argument. Let's look at the following examples:

e.g. 4. A: Every time Tom studies hard for a test, he gets a good grade.
　　　B: To continue to get good grades, therefore, he needs to continue to study hard for the coming test.

e.g. 5. A: Every time Tom fails in math, he gets punished by his mom.
　　　B: To avoid being punished by his mom, he has to pass math.

Both comparative argument and causal argument are inductive reasoning. It uses specific information that has been observed or experienced, and draws general conclusions about it. Because the conclusions can only state what is likely or probable, there is a greater chance of making a mistake in inductive reasoning.

e.g. 6. A: Ann smokes and she has lung cancer.

      B: Emily smokes and she has lung cancer.

      A: In fact, every smoker I know now has lung cancer.

      B: Therefore, if you smoke you will have lung cancer. (false)

In this case, we can only say:

e.g. 7. Therefore, if you smoke you will have a good chance of getting lung cancer. (true)

 ## How to Claim: Logic (II)

Lead-in Questions:

1. What is deduction?

2. What is a major premise?

3. What is a minor premise?

4. What is a syllogism?

5. What is conditional deduction?

e.g. 8. A: If you finish your supper, you will get some dessert.

      B: You finished your supper.

        You got some dessert.

We are familiar with the scene, and we grow up with this logic pattern. What is it? Let's find out the answer.

Here we move from the general principle to the specific case, and this is deductive reasoning. It is a mental process of moving from one statement through another to a conclusion. Deduction is the reasoning process of drawing a conclusion from two things that are known as general premises. Usually it includes three parts: a major premise, a minor premise, and a conclusion.

Naturally, the credibility of the deductive conclusion is based on the premises. The premises must be truthful facts, rules, laws, principles or generalizations.

Even just one word can change the premise from fact to fiction, such as the words "all" and "every".

e.g. 9. The major premise: All dogs are spotty.

      The minor premise: Bob is a dog.

      The conclusion: Bob is spotty.

In fact, only some dogs are spotty. The first premise is untrue, which makes the conclusion invalid.

8.3.1 Major Premise

A major premise is a statement of general truth dealing with categories rather than individual examples. Here are two examples of major premises:

e.g. 10. All women were once girls.

e.g. 11. Professors hold advanced degrees.

Have you noticed any important factors of a major premise? First, there are two parts in the premise, namely it relates to two terms. Second, a major premise describes something general. So, a major premise relates to two terms, and is stated as something general, such as a generalization, rule or principle.

8.3.2 Minor Premise

A minor premise is a specific example of the major premise. Look at the following two minor premises:

e.g. 12. My sister is a woman.

e.g. 13. Dr. Jackson is a professor.

"My sister" and "Dr. Jackson" are specific examples of the two general groups—women and professors.

8.3.3 Conclusion

The conclusions should be completely guaranteed and not just made probable by the truth of the premises. The conclusions must follow logically and not go beyond or make assumptions about the premises.

Now, let's have a try! Is the following a valid deductive reasoning or not?

e.g. 14. The major premise: Banks make money by charging interest.

The minor premise: My bank charges me interest.

The conclusion: My bank makes money.

Since there is no additional information, no assumptions or inferences are made. This is a valid deductive reasoning.

e.g. 15. The major premise: Ernest Hemingway wrote some great books.

The minor premise: Ernest Hemingway wrote *The Old Man and the Sea*.

The conclusion: *The Old Man and the Sea* is a great book.

As to this case, we may think it is a valid deductive reasoning. Yes, it is true that *The Old Man and the Sea* is a great book, but here the focus is whether the case is a valid deductive reasoning or not. Let's have a close look. The major premise states that some books are great, while the conclusion assumes that *The Old Man and the Sea* falls into that group. Actually, there is no evidence in the premises that this is true. This deduction is invalid.

Deductive reasoning has two forms. One is syllogism. As illustrated above, a syllogism is made up of two premises and a conclusion. The first premise describes a group (A), and a characteristic of that group (B). The second premise places a person or thing (C) within (A). The conclusion states that (C) is (B). Here comes the classic example of syllogisms.

e.g. 16. The major premise: Human beings are mortal.

The minor premise: Socrates is a human being.

The conclusion: Socrates is mortal.

A syllogism can take a positive or negative way, as in the following cases:

e.g. 17. The positive way:

The major premise: All vegetarians do not eat meat.

The minor premise: George is a vegetarian.

The conclusion: George does not eat meat.

e.g. 18. Or the negative way:

The major premise: All vegetarians do not eat meat.

The minor premise: George is not a vegetarian.

The conclusion: George eats meat.

The other form of deductive reasoning is conditional. The premise states that if something is true of A, then something is true of B. Here the pattern is "if A, then B".

e.g. 19. If you attend Health Club, you will lose weight. (If A, then B)

I attend Health Club. (A)

Therefore, I lose weight. (B)

Can you state the following statement as a syllogism and as a conditional deductive argument?

e.g. 20. Wherever his team wins, Ted gives a party. He will give a party tonight.

A syllogism is made up of two premises and a conclusion.

e.g. 21. The major premise: Each time the winning of the team means Ted gives a party.

The minor premise: The team wins.

The conclusion: Ted gives a party.

A conditional's pattern is "if A, then B".

e.g. 22. If the team wins, then Ted gives a party.

The team wins.

Therefore, Ted gives a party.

Deductive reasoning starts with the premise, which may be rules, laws, principles, or generalizations, and forms a conclusion based upon the premise. The premise must be true and the conclusion must follow the premise logically without trying to go beyond. In this way, we get a valid deductive argument.

How to Claim: Logic (III)

Lead-in Questions:

1. What is causal reasoning?

2. What is analogical reasoning?

Do you still remember the case: When students started wearing uniforms, their scores went up; therefore, uniforms improved their scores. And we also know that this is only a coincidence. Uniform wearing cannot be used as the evidence to support the conclusion. If we want to support ourselves with evidence, we have to know the relation between causes and effects, namely reasons and results.

Causes refer to "What happened? What are the possible reasons? Which is the most likely? Why?".

Effects refer to "What happened? Who was involved? What are the observable results? What are some possible future results?".

Point out the cause and effect respectively:

e.g. 23. You get a flat tire. You are late for class.

As we can see in Example 23, the first sentence is the cause, while the second one is the effect. Let's look at another example:

e.g. 24. Obsession with dieting; having a poor body image.

Is the first half of the sentence still the cause, the second half the effect? Or quite the opposite: Someone may be obsessed with dieting just because of his/her poor body image. In this case, we can call it mutual cause-effect relation.

Look at Example 25:

e.g. 25. Job changing means less pressure, higher pay, longer commuting time.

Example 25 is about one cause and multiple effects.

e.g. 26. Hardworking, persistence, parent's support—College admission

Example 26 is about one effect and multiple causes.

There may also be multiple causes multiple effects. Sometimes we have chains of causes and effects as shown in Example 27:

e.g. 27. You got up late.
       You were late for the interview. (effect, cause).

"You were late for the interview." can be both the effect from "You got up late." and the cause for "You missed a job position."

"You missed a job position." can be both the effect from "You were late for the interview." and the cause for "You are still under unemployment."

It is important to realize that the statements are not always stated using the words "cause" and "effect". Many other words and expressions similar in meaning are used, such as "produce" "bring about" "lead to" "generate", etc. to introduce the "effect". Can you find out some expressions for introducing the "cause"?

We challenge what has been said and then certify our challenge with evidence and logical reasoning to form a certain claim. Once the claim is made, it is open to be challenged. Evidence is collected and reasoning is made to certify the new challenge until we arrive at a new conclusion. Critical thinking is forever circling and that is why human beings move forward and go somewhere.

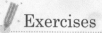

Exercises

I.　Mark true (T) or false (F) for the following statements.

1. Mind maps are effective ways to visualize our thoughts.　　　　　（　）

2. Mind maps mean drawing maps only in your own mind.　　　　　（　）

3. We claim not only about reality, truth, the way things are and also about values.（　）

4. Induction is the process of reasoning from something specific to something general.　　　　　　　　　　　　　　　　　　　　　（　）

5. A conclusion based upon correct premises always leads to a valid conclusion.　（　）

6. A major premise only describes a group.　　　　　　　　　（　）

7. Both comparative argument and causal argument are inductive reasoning.　（　）

8. A syllogism cannot take a negative way.　　　　　　　　　（　）

9. The relationship between causes and effects can be mutual and sometimes they even form chains.　　　　　　　　　　　　　　　（　）

10. Critical thinking, as a forever circling process, pushes human beings to move forward.　　　　　　　　　　　　　　　　　　　　（　）

II.　List at least three causes/effects for the following statements.

1. Cause: I joined the speech club two months ago.

　　Effects:

　　1) _____

　　2) _____

　　3) _____

2. Cause: lack of sleep

　　Effects:

　　1) _____

　　2) _____

　　3) _____

3. Cause: newly divorced

　　Effects:

　　1) _____

　　2) _____

　　3) _____

Part II

Topics for Effective Expression

Unit 1 — Learning

★ Text A
Learning to Learn

Organizations today are in constant flux. In the words of Arie de Geus, a business theorist, "The ability to learn faster than your competitors may be the only sustainable competitive advantage." Over decades of coaching and consulting to thousands of executives in a variety of industries, however, my colleagues and I have come across people who succeed at this kind of learning. We've identified four attributes they have in spades: aspiration, self-awareness, curiosity, and vulnerability. They truly want to understand and master new skills; they see themselves very clearly; they constantly think of and ask good questions; and they tolerate their own mistakes as they move up the learning curve.

Aspiration

It's easy to see aspiration as either there or not: You want to learn a new skill or you don't; you have ambition and motivation or you lack them. But great learners can raise their aspiration level—and that's the key, because everyone is guilty of sometimes resisting development that is critical to success.

When we do want to learn something, we focus on the positive—what we'll gain from learning it—and envision a happy future in which we're reaping those rewards. That propels us into action. Researchers have found that shifting your focus from challenges to benefits is a good way to increase your aspiration to do initially unappealing things. For example, when Nicole Detling, a psychologist at the University of Utah, encouraged aerialists and speed skaters to picture themselves benefiting from a particular skill, they were much more motivated to practice it.

Self-Awareness

Over the past decade or so, most leaders have grown familiar with the concept of self-awareness. But when it comes to the need for learning, our assessments of ourselves—what we know and don't know, skills we have and don't have—can still be woefully inaccurate. In one study conducted by David Dunning, a Cornell University psychologist, 94% of college professors reported that they were doing "above average work." Clearly, almost half were wrong—many extremely so—and their self-deception surely diminished any appetite for development. Only 6% of respondents saw themselves as having a lot to learn about being an effective teacher.

In my work I've found that the people who evaluate themselves most accurately start the process inside their own heads: They accept that their perspective is often biased or flawed and then strive for greater objectivity, which leaves them much more open to hearing and acting on others' opinions.

One CEO I know was convinced that he was a great manager and leader. He did have tremendous industry knowledge and great instincts about growing his business, and his board acknowledged those strengths. But he listened only to people who affirmed his view of himself and dismissed input about shortcomings; his team didn't feel engaged or inspired. When he finally started to question his assumptions ("Is everyone on my team focused and productive? If not, is there something I could be doing differently?"), he became much more aware of his developmental needs and open to feedback. He realized that it wasn't enough to have strategic insights; he had to share with them his reports and invite discussion, and then set clear priorities—backed by quarterly team and individual goals, regular progress checks, and troubleshooting sessions.

Curiosity

Kids are relentless in their urge to learn and master. As John Medina writes in Brain Rules, "This need for explanation is so powerfully stitched into their experience that some scientists describe it as a drive, just as hunger and thirst and sex are drives." Curiosity is what makes us try something until we can do it, or think about something until we understand it. Great learners retain this childhood drive, or regain it through another application of self-talk. Instead of focusing on and reinforcing initial disinterest in a new subject, they learn to ask themselves "curious questions" about it and follow those questions up with actions. Carol Sansone, a psychology researcher, has found, for example, that people can increase their willingness to tackle necessary tasks by thinking about how they could do the work differently to make it more interesting. In other words, they change their self-talk from "This is boring to I wonder if I could…"

Vulnerability

Once we become good or even excellent at some things, we rarely want to go back to being not good at other things. Great learners allow themselves to be vulnerable enough to accept that beginner state. In fact, they become reasonably comfortable in it—by managing their self-talk.

Generally, when we're trying something new and doing badly at it, we think terrible thoughts: "I hate this. I'm such an idiot. I'll never get this right. This is so frustrating!" That static in our brains leaves little bandwidth for learning. The ideal mindset for a beginner is both vulnerable and balanced: "I'm going to be bad at this to start with, because I've never done it before." And "I know I can learn to do it over time." In fact, the researchers Robert Wood and Albert Bandura found in the late 1980s that when people are encouraged to expect mistakes and learn from them early in the process of acquiring new skills, the result is "heightened interest, persistence, and better performance".

I know a senior sales manager from the United States who was recently tapped to run the Asia-Pacific region for his company. He was having a hard time acclimating to living overseas and working with colleagues from other cultures, and he responded by leaning on his sales expertise rather than acknowledging his beginner status in the new environment. I helped him recognize his resistance to being a cultural novice, and he was able to shift his self-talk from "This is so uncomfortable—I'll just focus on what I already know to I have a lot to learn about Asian cultures. I'm a quick study, so I'll be able to pick it up." He told me it was an immediate relief: Simply acknowledging his novice status made him feel less foolish and more relaxed. He started asking the necessary questions, and soon he was seen as open, interested, and beginning to understand his new environment.

The ability to acquire new skills and knowledge quickly and continually is crucial to success in a world of rapid change. If you don't currently have the aspiration, self-awareness, curiosity, and vulnerability to be an effective learner, these simple tools can help you get there.

(Source: Andersen, E. 2016, March 1. Learning to learn. *Harvard Business Review.*)

Effective Expression: A Linguistic Dimension ＼＼＼

The "4.1 Supporting Details" of Part I explains several kinds of supporting details including statistics, quotations, authoritative references and anecdotes. A clear statement plus supporting details helps make a strong argument, which is an important writing strategy in argumentation and exposition. *Text A* is an exposition aiming to explain the four essential attributes of success. Let's locate some supporting details and analyze their functions.

Original Texts	Supporting Details	Analyses
Organizations today are in constant flux. In the words of Arie de Geus, a business theorist, "The ability to learn faster than your competitors may be the only sustainable competitive advantage." (Paragraph 1)	✓ Quotation of Arie de Geus, a business theorist	This quotation means in this fast-changing business world, you have to learn faster than your competitors if you want to keep your competitive advantage in business. This quotation is to support the beginning sentence: "Organizations today are in constant flux." The two expressions "constant flux" and "sustainable competitive advantage" echo each other in meaning. Besides supporting the former sentence, this quotation also works as a transitional one that helps define the discussion scope and pave the way for the upcoming ideas. In the following text, "the ability to learn" will be decomposed into four specific abilities.
But when it comes to the need for learning, our assessments of ourselves—what we know and don't know, skills we have and don't have—can still be woefully inaccurate. In one study conducted by David Dunning, a Cornell University psychologist, 94% of college professors reported that they were doing "above average work." Clearly, almost half were wrong—many extremely so— and their self-deception surely diminished any appetite for development. Only 6% of respondents saw themselves as having a lot to learn about being an effective teacher. (Paragraph 4)	✓ Authoritative reference to the study done by David Dunning, a Cornell University psychologist ✓ Statistics from the study	In order to illustrate the idea "our assessments of ourselves can still be woefully inaccurate", the findings of the study conducted by a Cornell University psychologist were referred. Besides, specific numbers were presented such as 94%, almost half and 6% to make the details more accurate and convincing.

(cont.)

Original Texts	Supporting Details	Analyses
I know a senior sales manager from the United States who was recently tapped to run the Asia-Pacific region for his company. He was having a hard time acclimating to living overseas and working with colleagues from other cultures, and he responded by leaning on his sales expertise rather than acknowledging his beginner status in the new environment. I helped him recognize his resistance to being a cultural novice, and he was able to shift his self-talk from This is so uncomfortable—I'll just focus on what I already know to I have a lot to learn about Asian cultures. I'm a quick study, so I'll be able to pick it up. He told me it was an immediate relief: Simply acknowledging his novice status made him feel less foolish and more relaxed. He started asking the necessary questions, and soon he was seen as open, interested, and beginning to understand his new environment. **(Paragraph 10)**	✓**Anecdote** of the author and one of his clients	Anecdote means personal story. Since it involves personal experience, it can function to support the idea vividly. In this case, the author introduces how he helped a senior sales manager to accept his novice status in overseas environment. By admitting his vulnerability in the situation, the sales manager felt an immediate relief and more relaxed, thus being focused on solving the real problems that confronted him in the new environment.

Effective Expression: A Rhetorical Dimension

Rhetorical devices refer to some particular sentence structure, sound or pattern to invoke special reactions from the readers or the audience. Apart from what have been introduced in Part I, a special rhetorical device was employed in *Text A*—dialogismus. Derived from the Greek word *dialogos*, the literal meaning of dialogismus is conversation. As a rhetorical device, it means speaking in the role of another person so as to express his or her ideas. All examples of dialogismuses of *Text A* can be seen in the table on the next page. When the author was describing the story of someone else, the third person pronoun was suddenly switched to the first-person pronoun. But apparently, here the first person referred to the protagonist of the story rather than the author. By doing so, the thoughts of the protagonist were expressed directly. Besides, the use of the first-person pronoun would help engage the readers more and let them think about whether they had expressed the same or similar ideas as the protagonist. Hence, a conversation between the author or the protagonist and the readers was achieved.

1.　When he finally started to question his assumptions ("Is everyone on my team focused and productive? If not, is there something I could be doing differently?"), he became much more aware of his developmental needs and open to feedback.

(Paragraph 6)

2.　In other words, they change their self-talk from "This is boring to I wonder if I could…"

(Paragraph 7)

3.　Generally, when we're trying something new and doing badly at it, we think terrible thoughts: "I hate this. I'm such an idiot. I'll never get this right. This is so frustrating!"

(Paragraph 9)

4.　The ideal mindset for a beginner is both vulnerable and balanced: "I'm going to be bad at this to start with, because I've never done it before." And "I know I can learn to do it over time."

(Paragraph 9)

5.　I helped him recognize his resistance to being a cultural novice, and he was able to shift his self-talk from "This is so uncomfortable—I'll just focus on what I already know to I have a lot to learn about Asian cultures. I'm a quick study, so I'll be able to pick it up."

(Paragraph 10)

Effective Expression: A Logical Dimension ＼＼＼

According to "7.4 How to Certify (I): Evidence" of Part I, it is important to employ different types of evidence to certify effectively. But how do we choose valid evidence? The ARTS format was proposed before. ARTS stands for Accurate, Relevant, Typical and Sufficient respectively. Let's use the ARTS format to examine some evidence in *Text A*.

Original Text	The Features of the Evidence	Analyses
In one study conducted by David Dunning, a Cornell University psychologist, 94% of college professors reported that they were doing "above average work". Clearly, almost half were wrong—many extremely so—and their self-deception surely diminished any appetite for development. Only 6% of respondents saw themselves as having a lot to learn about being an effective teacher. (Paragraph 4)	Accurate	Some statistics from the study are provided, including "94%", "almost half" and "6%". Obviously, specific numbers speak louder.
	Relevant	As explained in the previous lexical dimension, this evidence was used to support the argument about the self-deception. The evidence is highly relevant.
	Typical	Typical means characteristic and representative of a certain category. This scientific evidence is typical enough to stand out and make sense of the argument.
	Sufficient	The specific results of a study conducted by a psychologist from Cornell University are convincing enough to make the point.

Interactive Writing

In *Text A*, the author argues that "The ability to learn faster than your competitors may be the only sustainable competitive advantage". How much do you agree or disagree with this opinion? Expound your ideas in NO LESS THAN 150 words.

You should pay attention to the relevance and sufficiency of the content, organization, and language quality.

_____

_____

_____

_____

_____

_____

★ Text B

Academic Motivations Can Change

Parents may fear that if their high school student isn't motivated to do well in classes, there's nothing that will change that. But a new study that followed more than 1,600 students over two years found that students' academic motivation often did change—and usually for the better. Results showed that increasing students' sense of "belongingness" in school was one key way of increasing academic motivation.

"Our results point to a more hopeful picture for students who start out with lower levels of motivation—they tend to shift toward more adaptive profiles with better motivational characteristics over time," said Kui Xie, lead author of the study and professor of educational studies at The Ohio State University. The study found that motivation was more complex than often assumed. Students often hold multiple types of motivation that drive their academic behavior. For example, some students may be motivated to do well in school by both their intrinsic love of learning, but also the desire to get a good job after graduation. Results placed students into six different profiles, from worst, which was amotivated—those who were not motivated at all—to best, autonomous motivated, meaning the student had an inner desire to learn, with no outside influence needed.

The study was published recently in the *Journal of Educational Psychology*. The study involved 1,670 students at 11 public high schools in central and northeastern Ohio who were in grades 9 to 11 when the study began. The students completed surveys that assessed their motivation in two consecutive school years. Motivation was measured by asking students how much statements like these described them: "I go to school because I experience pleasure and satisfaction while learning new things" and "I go to school because I need at least a high school diploma to find a high-paying job later on." School belongingness was measured the first year in a survey that asked students how true statements like this were for them: "I feel like a real part of this school."

Of the six motivation profiles, the researchers considered two of them maladaptive, two of them adaptive and two in the middle. The maladaptive profiles characterized students who had no motivation at all or were only motivated to go to school because they were forced.

"These are the students who are most at risk of dropping out if we can't find better ways to get them excited about school," said Xie, who heads Ohio State's Research Laboratory for Digital Learning. The two most adaptive profiles included students who were entirely motivated by their love of learning, or who combined love of learning with some external motivations, such as the desire to get into a good college. Many students did change their profiles between years one and two of the study. Depending on which profile they started in, between 40% and 77% changed. While students changed across all profiles, most often they switched to one of the adjacent profiles.

There was an overall positive change in students' motivation, results showed. For example, 8% of the students were in the most adaptive profile—autonomously motivated—in the first year, and that increased to 11.4% in the second year. The least adaptive profile, the amotivated, described 2.8% of the students in the first year, dropping to 2.1% in the second year. The other good news in the study was that the most adaptive motivational profiles tended to be the most stable as far as membership between years one and two, according to Xie.

"That means that if we can find better ways to motivate students, if we can get them in a better profile, they tend to stay there," he said.

Why did students tend to move in a positive direction in terms of motivation? "One reason may be simply because they're a year older and more developmentally mature," he said.

But the study did find two other factors that impacted how likely they were to become more motivated. One, not surprisingly, was prior achievement. Students who had higher grade point averages the first year were more likely to shift to or remain in profiles characterized by higher levels of academic motivation in year two of the study. The other factor was school belongingness, with students who felt they were more a part of their school in the first year being more likely to move to or stay in a more adaptive profile in the second year.

"This may be one area where we can help students become more motivated," Xie said. "Belongingness is something schools can change. They can find ways to help students feel like they are part of the school community." These results confirm those of a similar study by Xie and colleagues, published last year in the journal *Contemporary Educational Psychology*, that found the same six motivational profiles, plus one other, in a different, much larger sample of students. Because the previous study involved 10,527 students, it could identify a rarer profile that wasn't seen in this smaller sample size. Overall, both studies suggest that schools should routinely assess students' motivation in order to identify students who are most at risk for dropping out or underperforming. Then, schools can create personalized intervention programs that target students based on their motivational profile, he said. Most importantly, with a routine assessment plan on students' motivation, schools can implement interventions before students disengage or drop out from academic activities.

"When we design interventions, we should think about gradually shifting students to more adaptive profiles," Xie said. "We need to tailor the motivation strategies to specific profiles. There is no one universal strategy that will work for all groups."

(Source: Ohio State University. 2021, March 1. High school students tend to get more motivated over time: Study suggests feeling of belongingness key to improvement. *Science Daily.*)

Effective Expression in Practice ＼＼＼

1. Locate the signal words in the following text and then analyze their functions in the context respectively. An example has been given. (See "1.4 Signal Words" of Part I)

Original Text	Signal Words	Functions
Overall, both studies suggest that schools should routinely assess students' motivation in order to identify students who are most at risk for dropping out or underperforming. Then, schools can create personalized intervention programs that target students based on their motivational profile, he said. Most importantly, with a routine assessment plan on students' motivation, schools can implement interventions before students disengage or drop out from academic activities.	Overall	This summative word indicates that a summary of ideas will come along.

2. Keeping the consistency of pronouns helps make the ideas clearer and more concise. (See "2.1 Pronoun Clarity" of Part I) Check the use of pronouns in the following text to see what they refer to respectively.

" ① **This** may be one area where we can help students become more motivated," Xie said. "Belongingness is something schools can change. ② **They** can find ways to help students feel like ③ **they** are part of the school community." ④ **These** results confirm ⑤ **those** of a similar study by Xie and colleagues, published last year in the journal *Contemporary Educational Psychology*, that found the same six motivational profiles, plus one other, in a different, much larger sample of students. Because the previous study involved 10,527 students, ⑥ **it** could identify a rarer profile that wasn't seen in ⑦ **this** smaller sample size.	① : ＿＿＿＿＿＿＿＿ ② : ＿＿＿＿＿＿＿＿ ③ : ＿＿＿＿＿＿＿＿ ④ : ＿＿＿＿＿＿＿＿ ⑤ : ＿＿＿＿＿＿＿＿ ⑥ : ＿＿＿＿＿＿＿＿ ⑦ : ＿＿＿＿＿＿＿＿

3. Supporting details can appear in different forms. The "4.1 Supporting Details" of Part I introduces several types. List the supporting details for the arguments presented in the table below, and pay special attention to the expressions in bold.

Arguments	Supporting Details	Types of the Details
Students often hold **multiple types** of motivation that drive their academic behavior.		

(cont.)

Arguments	Supporting Details	Types of the Details
There was an **overall positive change** in students' motivation, results showed.		

4. The three Cs are the essential steps of critical thinking. The beginning paragraph of *Text B* is a good example of this format. Identify the three Cs of critical thinking in it. (See "7.1 Critical Thinking: The 3Cs Framework" of Part I)

① Parents may fear that if their high school student isn't motivated to do well in classes, there's nothing that will change that. ② But a new study that followed more than 1,600 students over two years found that students' academic motivation often did change—and usually for the better. ③ Results showed that increasing students' sense of "belongingness" in school was one key way of increasing academic motivation. **(Paragraph 1)**	① :_____ ② :_____ ③ :_____

Critical Thinking in Practice

Read the following excerpt carefully and comment on the topic in NO LESS THAN 150 words.

Is Motivation the Result of Action or the Cause of Action?

Scientists define motivation as your general willingness to do something. It is the set of psychological forces that compel you to take action. One of the most surprising things about motivation is that it often comes after starting a new behavior, not before. We have this common misconception that motivation arrives as a result of passively consuming a motivational video or reading an inspirational book. However, active inspiration can be a far more powerful motivator. Motivation is often the result of action, not the cause of it. Getting started, even in very small ways, is a form of active inspiration that naturally produces momentum. This effect is just like the Physics of Productivity because this is basically Newton's First Law applied to habit formation: Objects in motion tend to stay in motion. Once a task has begun, it is easier to continue moving it forward.

Unit 2　Social Connection

★ Text A
Weak-Tie Friendships May Mean More than You Think

For nearly 10 years, I have spent my Monday evenings attending rehearsals for my amateur choir. Mondays are not my favorite day, and I often arrive in a bad mood, but by the end of the rehearsal, I usually feel energized. The singing does me good. So do the people. With a few exceptions, I wouldn't describe my fellow choir members as close friends; most of them, I barely know at all. We exchange brief chats, smiles and the odd joke—but that's enough for me to come away feeling a little better about the world.

There is no choir practice now, and won't be for a long time. I miss it. In lockdown, I don't feel short on affection or emotional support, but I do feel short of friendly faces and casual conversations. Another way of putting this is that I miss my weak ties.

In 1973, Mark Granovetter, a sociology professor at Stanford University, published a paper entitled *The Strength of Weak Ties*. It went on to become one of the most influential sociology papers of all time. Until then scholars had assumed that an individual's well-being depended mainly on the quality of relationships with close friends and family. Granovetter showed that quantity matters, too.

One way to think about any person's social world is that you have an inner circle of people whom you often talk to and feel close with, and an outer circle of acquaintances whom you see infrequently or fleetingly. Granovetter named these categories "strong ties" and "weak ties". His central insight was that for new information and ideas, weak ties are more important to us than strong ones.

Granovetter surveyed 282 Boston-based workers and found that most of them got their jobs through someone they knew. But only a minority got the job through a close friend; 84% got their job through those weak-tie relationships—meaning casual contacts whom they saw only occasionally. As Granovetter pointed out, the people whom you spend a lot of time with swim in the same pool of information as you do. We depend on friendly outsiders to bring us news of opportunities from beyond our immediate circles—and so the more of those

acquaintances we have, the better.

The coronavirus pandemic may have a direct impact on people's weak ties, and the benefits they reap from them. Companies that have been forced to change working practices by the crisis may end up making a permanent shift toward home-working and virtual workspaces. Although workers stand to benefit in many ways, including increased flexibility, one possible downside of this change is that it shrinks our social networks.

Physical offices enable not only formal face-to-face meetings, but they also function as spaces for chance encounters with our professional weak ties—in other words, people with whom we do not work closely but whose work has an impact on our own.

Some companies specifically design their offices in order to generate serendipitous meetings among employees from different departments. This was the idea behind the Pixar building, the design of which was overseen by Steve Jobs. The building has a large central hall through which all employees have to pass several times a day. Jobs wanted colleagues to bump into each other, grab coffee and shoot the breeze. He believed in the power of these seemingly random conversations to fire up creativity.

Encounters with weak ties can be good for our mental wellbeing, too. When Gillian Sandstrom was living in Toronto as a graduate student in psychology, she often had to walk between two university buildings, passing a hotdog stand on the way. "I'd always smile and say hi to the hotdog lady," she says. "We never even had a conversation, but I felt recognized, I felt connected—and that made me feel good."

That episode inspired Sandstrom, now a senior lecturer in psychology at the University of Essex, to investigate the extent to which people derive happiness from weak-tie relationships. She asked a group of respondents to keep a record of all their social interactions over the course of several different days. She found that participants with larger networks of weak ties tended to be happier overall, and that on days when a participant had a greater number of casual interactions with weak ties—say, a local barista, a neighbor, a member of yoga class—they experienced more happiness and a greater sense of belonging.

Lockdown is making such encounters rarer for all of us. Weak-tie interactions happen when we are out and about, particularly when we're taking part in an activity of some kind, like singing or cycling. A 2016 study, for which psychologists recruited respondents from Italy and Scotland, showed that regardless of nationality or age, people who were members of groups such as sports teams or church communities enjoyed an increased sense of meaning and security. And the more groups of which they were members, the better.

Right now, most clubs and communal groups are banned from holding events, and may not be able to resume for a while. We're not regularly strolling down busy streets or bumping into people in cafés and bars. That means we're missing out on low-cost, low-stakes conversations. "Sometimes it's harder to talk to people we know well because those conversations come with an emotional burden," says Sandstrom. "Weak-tie conversations are lighter and less demanding."

For all these reasons, we should continue to try and find ways to cultivate weak-tie relationships, in lockdown and beyond. Even under conditions of social distancing, our more distant friends are important to us. "We're all curious to see how others are coping, what they're doing, to help us figure out how to behave," says Sandstrom.

Social media, she points out, is a useful substitute for weak-tie conversations. We can use it to reach out to people we don't know well for light, but meaningful interactions. She adds that we can also engage in more weak-tie-style interactions with our strong ties, checking to see how people are without engaging them in a full conversation. The goal, says Sandstrom, is to let others know you are thinking of them without asking for a great deal of time, energy or attention.

After this pandemic has passed, we should take care to rebuild our networks of casual acquaintances. We can learn a lot from talking to people we barely know.

(Source: BBC Editorial Team. 2020, July 1. Why your weak-tie friendships may mean more than you think. BBC.)

Effective Expression: A Linguistic Dimension

As the saying goes, a good beginning is half done. This is also true in writing, since a good start will attract the readers to continue reading. The "4.2 Introductions and Conclusions (I)" of Part I introduces several ways of starting an essay and the "4.3 Introductions and Conclusions (II)" explains several rules of ending an essay. Let's take a close look at the beginning and the ending of the text and review what has been discussed in Part I.

Original Texts	Analyses
Beginning: For nearly 10 years, I have spent my Monday evenings attending rehearsals for my amateur choir. Mondays are not my favorite day, and I often arrive in a bad mood, but by the end of the rehearsal, I usually feel energized. The singing does me good. So do the people. With a few exceptions, I wouldn't describe my fellow choir members as close friends; most of them, I barely know at all. We exchange brief chats, smiles and the odd joke—but that's enough for me to come away feeling a little better about the world. There is no choir practice now, and won't be for a long time. I miss it. In lockdown, I don't feel short on affection or emotional support, but I do feel short of friendly faces and casual conversations. Another way of putting this is that I miss my weak ties.	Paragraph 1 describes the 10-year routine on Mondays and how this routine has changed the author's mood and life. It is a good strategy to start with personal experience, since personal experience is filled with real emotions and specific details. Paragraph 2 describes the suspension of this routine due to the lockdown and this change makes the author feel short on emotional support. The last sentence leads to the key topic of this article—weak ties.
Ending: For all these reasons, we should continue to try and find ways to cultivate weak-tie relationships, in lockdown and beyond. Even under conditions of social distancing, our more distant friends are important to us. "We're all curious to see how others are coping, what they're doing, to help us figure out how to behave," says Sandstrom. Social media, she points out, is a useful substitute for weak-tie conversations. We can use it to reach out to people we don't know well for light, but meaningful interactions. She adds that we can also engage in more weak-tie-style interactions with our strong ties, checking to see how people are without engaging them in a full conversation. The goal, says Sandstrom, is to let others know you are thinking of them without asking for a great deal of time, energy or attention. After this pandemic has passed we should take care to rebuild our networks of casual acquaintances. We can learn a lot from talking to people we barely know.	"For all these reasons" indicates this article has come to the conclusion part. Since weak ties are important, the author calls on cultivating this weak-tie relationship despite the difficulties. Social media and weak-tie-style interactions with strong ties may be two solutions to the problem addressed in the article. The last sentence, quoted from Sandstrom, defines again weak-tie relationship without just copying the sentences before. The last paragraph echoes the title and the beginning of the article by looking ahead what we can do after the pandemic.

Effective Expression: A Rhetorical Dimension ⟍⟍⟍

In the "5.4 Metaphor" of Part I, we have discussed the core of metaphor, i.e. comparing two different objects to find the similarity between them. The comparison within a metaphor is implicit and implied. Such characteristic of metaphor reminds us of another figurative term: idiom. An idiom is a phrase or expression that typically presents a figurative, non-literal meaning attached to the phrase, i.e. the literal meaning has moved away from the original phrase. The non-literal meaning and the literal meaning share some similarities. Therefore, both metaphor and idiom involve finding something in common between two different things.

But you may wonder whether there is any difference between a metaphor and an idiom. The answer is yes. The difference between the two lies in the context. Since the comparison within a metaphor is indirect, the meaning of the metaphor relies much on the surrounding context. But an idiom does not require such context, because it has got its independent meaning through constant use. The meaning of the idiom has been recognized and accepted by the people in this language community. Let's examine the following three examples from *Text A*.

Original Texts	Figures of Speech
As Granovetter pointed out, the people whom you spend a lot of time with **swim in the same pool of information** as you do. We depend on friendly outsiders to bring us news of opportunities from beyond our immediate circles—and so the more of those acquaintances we have, the better. **(Paragraph 5)**	Metaphor: "Swim in the same pool of information" is compared to "spend a lot time together". Here "swim in the same pool of information" is a metaphor implying strong-tie relationships are usually exposed to the same information source.
Jobs wanted colleagues to **bump into** each other, grab coffee and **shoot the breeze**. **(Paragraph 8)**	Idioms: bump into: meet by chance shoot the breeze: spend time talking in an idle manner Apparently, the meanings of the two idioms are different from their literal meanings. Their meanings are set without depending much on the context.

Effective Expression: A Logical Dimension ⟍⟍⟍

From the "8.1 How to Certify (II): Mind Map" of Part I, we have learned five types of mind maps and their respective functions: circle maps, bubble maps, tree maps, brace maps and flow maps. Brace maps help us understand the relationship between a whole and its parts.

They are useful in analyzing the structure of an item. Here, let's try to use the brace map to illustrate the development of ideas of the article, i.e., the basic structure of *Text A*.

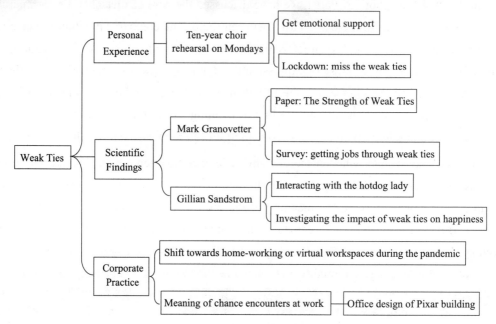

Figure 2–1　The Brace Map of Text A

Interactive Writing

Read carefully *Text A* and then summarize its main ideas in NO MORE THAN 100 words. You cannot copy sentences directly from the text, but you can use some expressions with no more than five words in a row.

Afterwards you should comment on the impact of technology on social network in NO LESS THAN 150 words. You can support your ideas with information from the text and/ or include any relevant examples from your own knowledge or experience. You should pay attention to the relevance and sufficiency of the content, organization and language quality.

_____

_____

_____

_____

_____

★ Text B

"Sorry, I Was Distracted..."

Have you ever been sitting around the dining table at home, completely immersed in Facebook and Instagram, and totally ignoring the world around you? Have you ever walked past a table at a restaurant where every person was looking down at his or her phone? Social disengagement and immersion in technology seems to be a common problem in modern society, particularly when it comes to friendships and relationships. In an age where we are constantly available to anyone who has our phone number, email address or Facebook details, it can be difficult to spend genuine, valuable time, actively engaged with our partner or friends in conversations and other shared activities. This constant connection using modern technology can create an illusion of increased connectivity, but at what cost?

Many of the communications we receive through our devices are superficial—alerts to view a distant acquaintance's holiday pics, ads from shops we once purchased from or charities we once donated $10 to. We also receive emails related to work, catching up with friends through a messaging service, or viewing some artistic photographs through Instagram. You may even be achieving level 132 on a game you have been working on in your spare time for a number of weeks.

This constant stimulation and abundance of digital social and leisure experiences may seem like a blessing—we no longer need to feel bored or as though we have nobody to communicate with. There is always a game to play, news story to read, photo album to browse or chat room to seek connection through. However, these experiences are presented to us in a medium that is designed to be addictive. Therefore, they often come at the expense of our real relationships. We can be constantly in contact with other people, but isolated and unfulfilled in our day-to-day life.

Many of the connections we build with people through the internet have a very different quality to them—there is an ease with which we can filter our lives and experiences on social media by posting only our most attractive photos, most interesting and impressive experiences and our wittiest thoughts. Through Facebook messenger stickers and emoticons, we can now have an entire digital conversation without writing many words at all. We may be happier with the image others are receiving of us, the person they are getting to know is a less authentic version. The person people know through the internet may not truly be us.

Social media has also affected our relationships because, by increasing the immediacy of communication, it has decreased our need for commitment. Gone are the days of landline phones, where a time and location are set well in advance, plans are made to facilitate being

able to attend the meeting and apologies are profuse if non-attendance occurs. Now, meeting times and places may not be decided until the last minute through a group chat, and "Maybe" is an acceptable RSVP option until an hour after the event started, at which point you are five episodes into the latest series of *House of Cards* and you really just want to know what happens next... "I'm too lazy to get ready now" might be a common reaction. In the end, this reduces our ability to consider options, make decisions and follow through with responsibilities.

The other effect of this increase in connectivity and activity is that we are never really alone and unoccupied anymore-because there is always a new post on Facebook to read, game to play or TV series to "binge watch", we are easily able to avoid confronting and processing negative internal experiences, and there is less need to engage in creative thought. This can play the role of maintaining psychological problems because we can so easily distract ourselves, avoid addressing the root of the issue and have less activities that leave us feeling fulfilled and accomplished, because most of our leisure time is spent consuming, rather than creating.

This new age of technology is an exciting one—there is so much information out there to learn and apply to our lives. However, it is important to consider the psychological costs of excessive technology use so that we can implement healthier patterns of device use and social interactions.

(Source: Strategic Psychology. 2021, March 1. "Sorry, I was distracted..."—The impact of technology on social connection. *Strategic Psychology.*)

Effective Expression in Practice ⟩⟩⟩

1. Comparison and contrast are commonly used to develop paragraphs (See "3.2 Comparison and Contrast" of Part I). Identify the comparison and contrast in Paragraph 5 of *Text B*.

Original Text	Comparison & Contrast
Social media has also affected our relationships because, by increasing the immediacy of communication, it has decreased our need for commitment. Gone are the days of landline phones, where a time and location are set well in advance, plans are made to facilitate being able to attend the meeting and apologies are profuse if non-attendance occurs. Now, meeting times and places may not be decided until the last minute through a group chat, and "Maybe" is an acceptable RSVP option until an hour after the event started, at which point you are five episodes into the latest series of *House of Cards* and you really just want to know what happens next... "I'm too lazy to get ready now" might be a common reaction. In the end, this reduces our ability to consider options, make decisions and follow through with responsibilities.	This paragraph describes how the social media has changed our social relationships. The relationships _____ have been _____ to the relationships _____. Some specific differences have been presented.

In the past	At present

2. Refer to "4.2 Introductions and Conclusions (I)" and "4.3 Introductions and Conclusions (II)" of Part I to analyze the beginning and the ending of *Text B*.

Original Texts	Analyses
Beginning: Have you ever been sitting around the dining table at home, completely immersed in Facebook and Instagram, and totally ignoring the world around you? Have you ever walked past a table at a restaurant where every person was looking down at his or her phone? Social disengagement and immersion in technology seems to be a common problem in modern society, particularly when it comes to friendships and relationships. In an age where we are constantly available to anyone who has our phone number, email address or Facebook details, it can be difficult to spend genuine, valuable time, actively engaged with our partner or friends in conversations and other shared activities. This constant connection using modern technology can create an illusion of increased connectivity, but at what cost?	

(cont.)

Original Text	Analysis
Ending: This new age of technology is an exciting one—there is so much information out there to learn and apply to our lives. However, it is important to consider the psychological costs of excessive technology use so that we can implement healthier patterns of device use and social interactions.	

3. "4.4 Body Paragraphs" of Part I explains the differences between Deductive Order and Inductive Order. The Deductive Order starts with a general statement and develops with specific details, and the Inductive Order is the opposite. Find one paragraph for each order from *Text B* and point out the general statement, i.e., the topic sentence.

Paragraphs	Orders of Developing Ideas	Topic Sentences
	_____ Order	
	_____ Order	

4. According to "6.3 Parallelism and Antithesis" of Part I, parallelism is a literary device in which parts of the sentence are grammatically the same, or are similar in construction. It can be a word, a phrase, or an entire sentence repeated. There is a repetition of a set of grammatical structures to show that a pair or list of ideas have equal weight or share equal importance. Identify at least two cases of parallelism in *Text B*.

1)

2)

3)

Critical Thinking in Practice ◥◥◥

Read the following excerpt carefully and comment on the topic in NO LESS THAN 150 words.

Will Human Interaction Strengthen or Suffer in the Digital Era?

The world is becoming increasingly digital. We do our shopping online, build our businesses online, spend our downtime online, and even make life-long friends online. As in July 2020, 59 percent of the global population were active Internet users. Bringing us closer to commodities, the Internet is set to become an even bigger part of our lives.

Technology is a fast-paced market, and every pioneer is in a race for the first place on the podium. New innovations are piloted every day in a desperate attempt to sell what the masses will buy to make our daily lives easier. As older generations warm to the idea of utilizing technology in the face of a pandemic, we move eerily closer to a world where social interaction is primarily digital. But should we look at this as a positive or negative change? Will human interaction strengthen or suffer as a result of new communication technologies?

Unit 3 Human Traits

★ Text A
The Power of Grit

Angela Duckworth, a professor at the University of Pennsylvania, was teaching seventh grade math in New York City public schools when she noticed that her best students were not necessarily her smartest students. The realization prompted her to leave her middle school classroom and become a research psychologist so she could better understand the role that foundational skills like self-control and perseverance play in achievement. Duckworth and her team studied children and adults in challenging environments, including West Point military cadets, national spelling bee contestants, and rookie teachers in difficult schools. In each study, she and her research team asked the same question: "Who is successful here and why?" Across numerous contexts, one characteristic emerged as a significant predictor of success: grit.

Grit is a psychological trait which is termed as positive and non-cognitive based on the person's perseverance and resolution to achieve goals in life. It is an amalgamation of passion and effort which states the determination for the long-term life goals and achievements. To measure grit, Duckworth and her team developed the "Grit Scale", a self-reported questionnaire used to evaluate focused effort and interest over time with questions such as, "I have overcome setbacks to conquer an important challenge." Respondents answer on a scale of one to five, with one being "not at all like me", and five being "very much like me". Once an individual completes the survey, his or her grit score can be calculated and used to determine how grit relates to other measures of success. In all those very different contexts, one characteristic emerged as a significant predictor of success. And it wasn't social intelligence. It wasn't good looks, physical health, and it wasn't I.Q. It was grit.

To many, grit is no news. The 99% perspiration, as mentioned in Edison's saying "Genius is 1% inspiration and 99% perspiration", is grit-tough-mindedness, perseverance, and hard work. Duckworth carried out extensive research in this domain and finally drew out that grit is the outcome of four ingredients: deliberate practice, interest, purpose, and hope. The light will be shed on each of these ingredients.

Setting out challenges for yourself and trying to break your records is what defines deliberate practice. The people with grittiness set onboard with the intention of not looking back with dissatisfaction but to look forward with utmost eager and want to grow. This is deliberate practice. This includes the people who have almost achieved their goals but are unable to satiate their hunger of growing and flourishing. Such people don't want to do well in the area they already do well in. Instead, they focus on their weaknesses and try to overcome them. They set out their challenges intentionally and then try to work hard for them. One can only improve if deliberate challenges are set. So, this is a kind of intensive practice that polishes the expert. A psych writer, Malcolm Gladwell, put forward a 10,000-hour rule which was based on the principle that to master in any field, at least 10,000 hours of deliberate practice is needed.

Importance of perseverance is one half of the equation. The other half is the interest, and passion found entangled with the efforts and hard work. The people who have a higher measure of grittiness have so much interest in their domain that the question related to it are all the time flashing in their minds. They go to sleep and wake up in the morning with the same flashing questions. Their minds are so clung to the domains of their interests that it is almost impossible to detach them from it. Therefore, to increase the capacity of grit in one's personality, it is essential to develop and enhance the interest. And the first part of this process is to find the importance and then make it consistent over the period. Interest is not developed suddenly out of nowhere. In fact, it needs to be evoked again, and again. People with high grit do the same, and then for keeping the interest active, they ask questions within questions. It is essential to foster the passion and then produce it in the form of benefits. That is the second ingredient of Grittiness.

The third element put forth by Duckworth is purpose and the desire to help others. Interest without purpose is nearly impossible to sustain for a lifetime. Angela has found while most people start out with a relatively self-orientated interest, as they learn self-disciplined practice, they start to appreciate how what they're doing might benefit others. If you already have a well-established interest, how might this make a positive difference for others? Gritty people are selfless. They think far beyond their existence. Psychologists Amy Wisniewski and Barry Schwartz did an extensive research about how people are successful in finding a purpose to their life and the desire to help others. The gritty people try to incorporate both interest and purpose in their passion. In the paradigm of GRIT, the purpose is not a mere ordinary purpose. It has a deeper meaning that surpasses self and goes beyond just goal orientation.

The last element of Grittiness is hope. According to Angela, the kind of hope associated with grit is a different kind of hope. "I hope that tomorrow will be a good day" differs from "I

am determined to make tomorrow a good day". The latter one characterizes hope associated with grit. According to Angela, gritty people do not rely on luck for what is going to happen next. They make their luck get forged through hard work and effort. In the process of understanding hope, it is imperative not to over-react on the failures and setbacks one gets. Instead, they should be tried to overcome in the best possible way.

(Sources: Anderson, K. & Francisco, A. 2019, March 6. The research behind the TED Talk: Angela Duckworth on grit. *Digital Promise*.

Arsalan. 2019. Angela Duckworth: The power of grit. Retrieved June 1, 2023, from Academic Master website.

Wondrlust. 2019. Interest, practice, purpose, hope: Is grit over-rated? Retrieved June 1, 2023, from Wondrlust website.)

Effective Expression: A Linguistic Dimension ＼＼＼

In expository writing, the author develops one or several paragraphs to inform the audience of a subject or a concept. To provide clear information in an organized way, there are several patterns of development. They are **definition** (when the author defines a term or concept in detail), **comparison and contrast** (when the author explores similarities and differences between two subjects), **cause and effect** (when the author conducts a causal analysis), **classification** (when the author explains a subject or term by dividing it into categories), and **process analysis** (when the author gives information about how to do or make something). "3.2 Comparison and Contrast" of Part I illustrates the development pattern of comparison and contrast. Now, let's explore another pattern, definition, which is employed several times in *Text A*.

In a short essay, a definition is provided to explain a key term or concept in detail. When do we use definitions? When the key term is essential for audience to understand and when it might not be quite commonly seen, it is necessary to provide a definition. Like in *Text A*, as indicated in the title, grit is the key term. To most audience, however, it is not as familiar a trait as patience or honesty.

There can be a sentence definition and an extended definition, depending on the purpose and length of the essay. A sentence definition usually begins with the term to be defined followed by a be verb, a general class the term belongs to, and features that differentiate it from the rest of others in the same class. The latter half of the sentence is usually in the form of a relative or appositive clause. For example:

- Vlog is a blog that contains video material.

In this definition, Vlog is the term to be defined. Blog is the general class it belongs to. What makes it different from other blogs is that it contains video material. In the text, the second paragraph begins with a definition developed in the structure.

- Grit is a psychological trait which is termed as positive and non-cognitive based on the person's perseverance and resolution to achieve the goals in life.

Clearly, grit is the term to be defined. It's a psychological trait, which is a general class grit belongs to. In the relative clause, grit is further defined as "positive and non-cognitive" in nature and its differentiating features are "perseverance and resolution to…".

Sometimes, a sentence definition consists of other patterns like a dash (-) or phrases like "refers to" and "is defined/termed as". For example:

- The 90% perspiration, as mentioned in Einstein's saying "Genius is 10% inspiration and 90% perspiration", is grit-tough-mindedness, perseverance, and hard work.
- A self-reported questionnaire refers to one of the most widely used assessment strategies in clinical psychology.

The following are two problems we should avoid when providing a sentence definition. First, don't overuse dictionary/encyclopedia definitions. Novice writers tend to copy dictionary definition, which is neither intriguing nor innovative. It is about as helpful as beginning an essay with "With the development of science and technology…". Second, avoid circular definitions. "An accountant is the person who does accounting." This is merely renaming or paraphrasing the term. We should explain it.

In essay writing, an extended definition can be provided in several sentences or paragraphs. There are several strategies we can employ to define a term or concept.

First, we can explain in detail the characteristics and the class the term belongs to. The second paragraph of *Text A* is a typical example of extended definition with detailed description of its features and other technicalities. Such features of grit as passion, determination, and long-term are mentioned in the sentence beginning with "It is an amalgamation of…". The rest of the paragraph is about how it is measured in the studies and concluded as an indicator of success.

Second, we can compare the term to or contrast it with other terms. In the last but second paragraph of *Text A*, the author intends to expound on the third element of grittiness proposed by Duckworth—purpose. To most people, they live a life of purpose, or "a relatively self-orientated interest". Gritty people, in contrast, have in mind a purpose not just for "their (own) existence", but one that "benefits others" and "surpasses self and goes beyond just goal orientation". The sense of "purpose and desire to help" is what defines people with grit. Some experienced writers describe the process as negation. They define the term by explaining what it doesn't mean, like in the text, "not a mere ordinary purpose".

Third, we can analyze causes and effects. When we finish reading *Text A* about grit and the four essential elements of it, we might wonder what we can do to foster grit in ourselves. Some researchers propose the idea of "growth mindset". Angela Duckworth argues in a TED talk:

The best idea I've heard about building grit in kids is something called "growth mindset". This is an idea developed at Stanford University by Carol Dweck, and it is the belief that the ability to learn is not fixed, that it can change with your effort. Dr. Dweck has shown that when kids read and learn about the brain and how it changes and grows in response to challenge, they're much more likely to persevere when they fail, because they don't believe that failure is a permanent condition.

In the passage, Angela Duckworth begins with a typical sentence definition in "it is the belief that…". She moves on to analyze what may happen to kids when they are taught the idea of "growth mindset"—they become "more likely to persevere".

Fourth, we can provide some examples and case studies to help readers understand the term or concept. In the same TED talk, Angela Duckworth explains the idea of grit as a predictor of success by describing how she and her team conducted their research:

My research team and I went to West Point Military Academy. We tried to predict which cadets would stay in military training and which would drop out. We went to the National Spelling Bee and tried to predict which children would advance farthest in competition… We partnered with private companies, asking, which of these salespeople is going to keep their jobs? And who's going to earn the most money?

Fifth, we can explore the origin or history of the term or concept. The strategy is especially helpful when a relatively new term is to be defined. For example:

Originally used by anthropologists to describe self-perpetuating processes that keep agrarian societies from progressing, involution has become a shorthand used by Chinese urbanites to describe the ills of their modern lives: Parents feel intense pressure to provide their children with the very best; children must keep up in the educational rat race; office workers have to clock in a grinding number of hours.

In expository writing, we can adopt one or, more often than not, a combination of two or three of the above strategies to make a clear and logical definition.

Effective Expression: A Rhetorical Dimension

In "5.2 Alliteration, Assonance, and Consonance" of Part I, a rhetorical device is introduced, consonance. Consonance is repetition of sounds in quick succession produced by consonants within a sentence or phrase. The repetitive sound is often found in the middle or at the end of a word. To put it simply, consonance is the repetition of internal and ending consonant sounds. An example in *Text A* is the very famous saying by Thomas Edison about genius, "Genius is 1% inspiration and 99% perspiration." Note that two key terms in the saying "inspiration" and "perspiration" contain sounds of similar consonants in very close proximity.

The saying itself is another very commonly seen rhetorical and literary device, aphorism. Aphorism is a statement of truth or opinion expressed in a concise and witty manner. It's concise and easy to remember, mainly because it employs some of the phonological rhetorical devices, as mentioned in "5.1 A Brief Introduction to Rhetoric and Rhetorical Devices" of Part I. The combination of similar sounds creates a pleasant rhythm to readers' ears. Aphoristic sayings are often quoted in writings and public speeches. They impart wisdom of truth handed down by tradition from generation to generation. Some best-known examples of aphorism on grit are as follows. Read them aloud and feel the rhythm.

- Our greatest glory is not in never falling, but in rising every time we fall.

  — Confucius

- What does it take to be the first female anything? It takes grit, and it takes grace.

  — Meryl Streep

- True grit is making a decision and standing by it, doing what must be done.

  — John Wayne

- Austere perseverance, hash and continuous... rarely fails of its purpose, for its silent power grows irresistible greater with time.

  — Johann Wolfgang Von Goethe

- Success consists of getting up just one more time than you fall.

  — Oliver Goldsmith

- Success is not final, failure is not fatal: It is the courage to continue that counts.

  — Winston Churchill

Quoting aphoristic sayings is a quick way to help readers relate to the message a writer intends to deliver, because they usually include a truth of universal acceptance. But don't overuse them because our original ideas and our unique way of organizing ideas are what make our essay impressive.

Effective Expression: A Logical Dimension

In "8.1 How to Certify (II): Mind Map" of Part I, several major types of mind maps are introduced. To create mind maps is an important learning strategy to organize information. When we read an essay, it's important to be able to identify its structure and key information. A mind map would be the easiest way to help us retrieve information without referring to the original essay. It contains keywords, colors, arrows, and other signs and symbols to visualize key information and structure, and how key points are associated with each other. Below is a mind map developed by a student. Compare it with *Text A* and see if it covers all the major points and reflects how the key points work together to support the main argument.

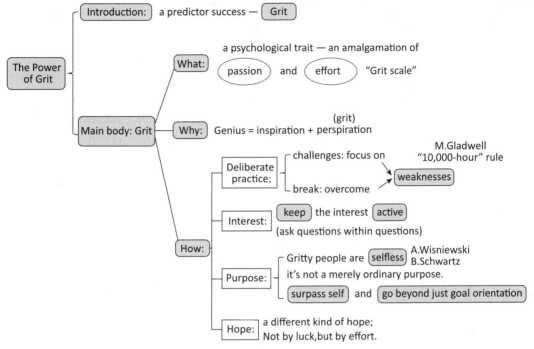

Figure 3–1　The Mind Map Developed by a Student

Interactive Writing

Read *Text A* carefully and comment on the topic of grit in NO LESS THAN 150 words.

- Do you believe grit is a predictor of success? To what extent? In which field?
- Do the "four ingredients" (deliberate practice, interest, purpose, and hope) play an equal role in making grit?

You can support yourself with information from the text and/or include any relevant examples from your own knowledge or experience. You should pay attention to the relevance and sufficiency of the content, organization and language quality.

_____

_____

_____

_____

_____

★ Text B
Angela Duckworth Responds to a New Critique of Grit

Grit expresses the idea that a crucial component of success is people's ability to pick a goal and stick with it. That's the main thrust of research by Angela Duckworth at the University of Pennsylvania. But a new report suggests that we should all take a step back and chill. The study, Much Ado About Grit: A Meta-Analytic Synthesis of the Grit Literature, analyzes 88 separate studies by Duckworth and others. "My overall assessment is that grit is far less important than has commonly been assumed and claimed," says the lead author, Marcus Crede, an assistant professor of psychology at Iowa State University. "And it doesn't tell us anything that we don't already know."

Here are the key claims in Crede's paper:

1. Effect sizes in one of Duckworth's major papers on grit were described incorrectly to sound misleadingly large.

2. The impact of grit is exaggerated, especially when looking at broader populations of people-not just the high achievers in Duckworth's initial studies.

3. Grit is nearly identical to conscientiousness, which has been known to psychologists for decades as a major dimension of personality. It is not something that's necessarily open to change, especially in adults, whereas Duckworth in her writings suggests that grit is.

On Point No.1, Duckworth admits to the charge of badly describing the size of her outcomes. In a 2009 paper, she and co-author Patrick Quinn famously looked at answers by West Point cadets on an eight-item version of her "grit scale". The paper stated that grit was highly predictive of the likelihood of making it through "Beast Barracks", or basic training. "Cadets who scored a standard deviation higher than average on the Grit-S were 99% more likely to complete summer training," the paper says.

That sure sounds like a big win for grit. But, as Crede points out, in fact what happened is that 95 percent of all cadets make it through Beast Barracks, while 98 percent of the very "grittiest" candidates made it through. This is a technical point, but to simplify, it's the odds of making it through that improved by 99 percent. Most laypeople, though, would interpret "99% more likely" as meaning that your chances of getting through bounced, say, from 40 percent to 80 percent. Not by 3 percentage points. The correct numbers are clear from the charts and tables in the original paper. Duckworth, in an email, agreed with the critique. "Crede is right that I should have said [it that way]... but again, the tables and statistics are entirely correct, and the intent was not to mislead!"

On Point No.2, Crede's paper calls the relationship between grit and academic success "only modest". His analysis found an overall correlation of 0.18, looking at papers by Duckworth and others. This compares to a much higher correlation of 0.50 between, say, SAT scores and performance in college. Duckworth's own numbers, in a paper published in 2007, are only slightly higher: 0.20. Fundamentally, she told NPR Ed, she doesn't disagree with Crede here either. She says her findings of the independent impact of grit are what personality psychologists would put in the "small-to-medium" range.

Point No.3 is in some ways Crede's biggest. He's challenging the uniqueness of grit, and therefore its usefulness as an object of research. The search for a scientific way to describe personality traits goes back at least to the 1930s. But in recent decades, psychologists have settled on a group of personality dimensions known as the Big Five: conscientiousness, agreeableness, extroversion, neuroticism and openness. Components of conscientiousness include organization, self-control, thoughtfulness and goal-directed behavior. In the various studies Crede looks at, conscientiousness scores and grit scores are very highly correlated—between 80 and 98 percent. Therefore, he calls grit a case of "old wine in new bottles". This matters, because a major implication of Duckworth's work is that grit is a skill. Schools and districts around the country are currently working hard on creating curricula for grit, and even accountability tests to measure it. But, psychologists say conscientiousness isn't a skill. It's a trait—driven by some unknowable combination of genetics and environment. It can change, typically improving as children grow up, but it's not necessarily amenable to direct instruction. Nor would we necessarily wish it to be. "I think as a parent I would feel uncomfortable if my daughter came home and said, 'My school is changing my personality' ", Crede says.

Duckworth counters that some grit-targeted instructional interventions have, in fact, proved successful in experiments, particularly those that target growth mindset—and that teach about the importance of certain study techniques, like deliberate practice. Duckworth said in her response to Crede's paper that she would prefer to think of grit as "a member of the conscientiousness family", but one with independent predictive powers. One of the ways that Duckworth and other researchers have tried to distinguish grit from conscientiousness is by adding in a factor called "consistency of effort". In other words, gritty people tend to have a singular passion that they pursue year-in and year-out, accumulating "10,000 hours" of deliberate practice toward a point of utter mastery. Nope, argues Crede. When you look at people's responses to questions about consistency alone, he writes, they aren't predictive of very much at all. Not only that, he suggests that consistency may not help people under all circumstances. People with a monomaniacal obsession and superhuman powers of dedication are not the only model for success. After all, we don't all aspire to be Army generals or to win the spelling bee. Sometimes, in the face of a novel or creative challenge, you have to abandon your original approach, try something new, and ask for help. For example, Crede cites no less a

figure than Einstein, who is one of Duckworth's models of grit. "He almost got scooped on his big discovery, because he needed to ask for help with his math."

So, has the impact of grit been exaggerated? Or did something get lost in translation? Is it time to give up on grit and try something new? Duckworth says she never tried to oversell her findings, and has always tried to be "clear and honest". "I aspire to be a scientist who remains open to criticism because I can't possibly be 100% right about everything!" she told NPR Ed. She said she's currently thinking about revising her "grit scale", her basic experimental tool, specifically the questions about passion.

(Source: Kamenetz, A. 2016. MacArthur "Genius" Angela Duckworth responds to a new critique of grit. Retrieved June 1, 2023, from NPR website.)

Effective Expression in Practice ⟩⟩⟩

1. List all the words and related expressions from both *Text A* and *Text B* which mean "to be determined / determination to achieve something" or qualities required to do so. (See "1.2 Lexical Diversity" of Part I)

Words

_____

Expressions

_____

2. In "2.4 Syntactic Variety" of Part I, we learned that syntactic variety is an important technique we should master. To achieve variety, we can vary sentence length and structure, sentence beginnings, and combine different types of sentences. Find examples from both *Text A* and *Text B* to fill in the table below.

	Techniques	Examples	Analyses
1	Sentence length and structure		
2	Sentence beginnings		
3	Types of sentences		

3. The two texts in this unit present scientific studies on the same topic, but with different findings and claims. In *Text B*, a term in statistical studies, meta-analysis, is introduced, and some key claims from the study are discussed later in the text. Do some research and provide a definition of "meta-analysis". And then give a definition of grit based on what you have read in the texts and your personal experience.

Meta-analysis

_____

_____

The definition of grit

_____

_____

4. In "5.1 A Brief Introduction to Rhetoric and Rhetorical Devices" of Part I, we explore the three pillars of persuasion proposed by the ancient Greek philosopher, Aristotle. They are the appeals of ethos, pathos, and logos. Find in *Text B* how Marcus Crede employs different strategies to make strong arguments.

Appeal of ethos

_____

_____

_____

Appeal of pathos

_____

_____

_____

Appeal of logos

_____

_____

_____

5. In "7.1 Critical Thinking: The 3Cs Framework" of Part I, the 3Cs framework of critical thinking is proposed, which helps us make sensible judgments. To be a person aware of critical thinking, we begin with challenging what we read or see, and we move on to look for evidence to support our doubts, so that at the end we are able to make our own claims. *Text B* is fundamentally an example of how to follow the 3Cs framework. Fill in the table below to complete the process of critical thinking and make sensible judgments.

	Challenging	Certifying	Claiming
1			Effect sizes in one of Duckworth's major papers on grit were described incorrectly to sound misleadingly large.
2			The impact of grit is exaggerated.
3			Grit is nearly identical to conscientiousness

Critical Thinking in Practice

According to Angela Duckworth, gritter students are more likely to make bigger academic achievements. Is grit the only trait that matters in making a good student? Read the following illustration about some latest findings from a research and comment on important factors in making a good student in NO LESS THAN 150 words. You should give specific reasons and evidence to support your argument, including examples, research, logic, or knowledge from your own experience.

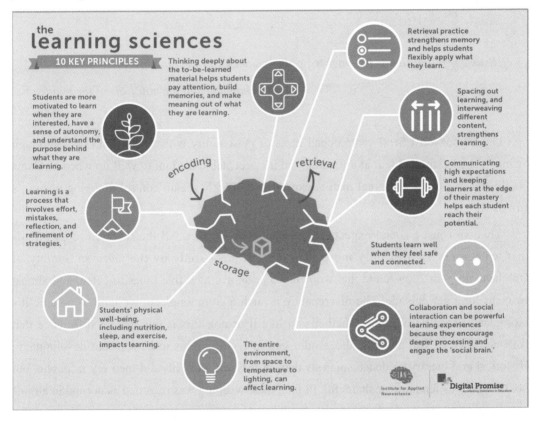

Unit 4　Gender Issues

Text A
Man, Weeping

History is full of sorrowful knights, sobbing monks and weeping lovers.

—What happened to the noble art of the manly cry?

One of our most firmly entrenched ideas of masculinity is that men don't cry. Although he might shed a discreet tear at a funeral, and it's acceptable for him to well up when he slams his fingers in a car door, a real man is expected to quickly regain control. Sobbing openly is strictly for girls.

This isn't just a social expectation; it's a scientific fact. All the research to date finds that women cry significantly more than men. A meta-study by the German Society of Ophthalmology in 2009 found that women weep, on average, five times as often, and almost twice as long per episode. The discrepancy is such a commonplace, we tend to assume it's biologically hard-wired; that, whether you like it or not, this is one gender difference that isn't going away. But actually, the gender gap in crying seems to be a recent development. Historical and literary evidence suggests that, in the past, not only did men cry in public, but no one saw it as feminine or shameful. In fact, male weeping was regarded as normal in almost every part of the world for most of recorded history.

Consider Homer's *Iliad*, in which the entire Greek army bursts into unanimous tears no less than three times. King Priam not only cries but tears his hair and grovels in the dirt for woe. Zeus weeps tears of blood, and even the immortal horses of Achilles cry buckets at the death of Patroklos. Of course, we can't regard the *Iliad* as a faithful account of historical events, but there's no question that ancient Greeks saw it as a model for how heroic men should behave. This exaltation of male weeping continued into the Middle Ages, where it appears in historical records, as well as fictional accounts. In chronicles of the period, we find one ambassador repeatedly bursting into tears when addressing Philip the Good, and the entire audience at a peace congress throwing themselves on the ground, sobbing and groaning as they listen to the speeches. Furthermore, the sobbing male hero wasn't only a Western phenomenon; he appears in Japanese epics as well. In *The Tale of Heike*, which is often cited as a source for the ideal behaviour of a samurai, we find men crying demonstratively at every turn. Here's a typical response to the death of a commander-in-chief: "Of all who heard, friend or foe, not one but wept until his sleeves were drenched."

Some might object that these are all public, ceremonial expressions of grief. Men might cry in this ritual manner over weighty issues of death, war and politics, but surely personal tears of love and frustration were still confined to women?

In a word, no. In medieval romances, we find innumerable instance of knights crying purely because they miss their girlfriends. In Chrétien de Troyes' *The Knight of the Cart*, no less a hero than Lancelot weeps at a brief separation from Guinevere. At another point, he cries on a lady's shoulder at the thought that he won't get to go to a big tournament. What's more, instead of being disgusted by this snivelling, she's moved to help.

Still more remarkably, there's no mention of the men in these stories trying to restrain or hide their tears. No one pretends to have something in his eye. No one makes an excuse to leave the room. They cry in a crowded hall with their heads held high. Nor do their companions make fun of this public blubbing; it's universally regarded as an admirable expression of feeling. Rampant male boo-hooing persisted well into the Early Modern period, and extended to parliamentarians as well as knights and monks.

So where did all the male tears go? The truth is, we don't know for certain. There was no anti-crying movement. No treatises were written against men's tears, and no leaders of church or state introduced measures to discourage them. Their decline occurred so slowly and quietly that no one seems to have noticed it happening. By the romantic period, masculine tears were reserved for poets. From here, it's just a short leap to the poker-faced heroes of Ernest Hemingway, who, despite their poetic leanings, cannot express grief by any means but tippling and shooting the occasional buffalo.

The most obvious possibility is that this shift is the result of changes that took place as we moved from a feudal, agrarian society to one that was urban and industrial. In the Middle Ages, most people spent their lives among those they had known since birth. A typical village had only 50-300 inhabitants, most of them related by blood or marriage. Men cried, but with empathetic friends and family around.

But from the 18th through the 20th centuries, the population became increasingly urbanised; soon, people were living in the midst of thousands of strangers. Furthermore, changes in the economy required men to work together in factories and offices where emotional expression and even private conversation were discouraged as time-wasting. As Tom

Lutz writes in *Crying: The Natural and Cultural History of Tears* (1999), factory managers deliberately trained their workers to suppress emotion with the aim of boosting productivity: "You don't want emotions interfering with the smooth running of things."

However, human beings weren't designed to swallow their emotions, and there's reason to believe that suppressing tears can be hazardous to your wellbeing. Research in the 1980s by Margaret Crepeau, then Professor of Nursing at Marquette University in Milwaukee, found a relationship between a person's rate of stress-related illnesses and inadequate crying. Weeping is also, somewhat counter-intuitively, correlated with happiness. Vingerhoets, a professor of psychology at Tilburg University in the Netherlands, has found that in countries where people cry the most, they also report the highest levels of satisfaction. Finally, crying is an important tool for understanding one's own feelings. A 2012 study of patients with Sjögren's syndrome—whose sufferers are incapable of producing tears—found they had significantly more difficulty identifying their emotions than a control group.

It's time to open the floodgates. Time for men to give up emulating the stone-faced heroes of action movies and be more like the emotive heroes of Homer, like the weeping kings, saints and statesmen of thousands of years of human history. When misfortune strikes, let us all—men and women—join together and cry until our sleeves are drenched. As the *Old Testament* has it: "They that sow in tears shall reap in joy."

(Source: Newman, S. 2015. Man, weeping. Retrieved June 1, 2023, from Aeon website.)

Effective Expression: A Linguistic Dimension ⟍⟍⟍

Section I

In "1.2 Lexical Diversity" of Part I, we learned that lexical diversity is an important indicator of a good command of English. In most English proficiency tests, like TOEFL and IELTS, lexical diversity is considered an essential aspect in grading rubrics.

In an essay about "crying", there must be a wide array of words and related expressions about "crying". They are listed as follows:

- **Words**

weep, sob, groan, snivel, blubbing, boohoo

- **Related Expressions**

sorrowful, shed a discreet tear, well up, burst into mountainous tears, weep tears, cry buckets, throw themselves on the ground, weep until one's sleeves are drenched, expression of grief, weighty issues of death, personal tears of love and frustration, miss their girlfriends, a brief separation, restrain or hide one's tears, emotional expression, suppress emotion, suppress tears, hazardous to one's wellbeing, stress-related illnesses, inadequate crying, open the floodgates, misfortune

Note that to put down all the expressions does not equal a mastery of them, let alone to be able to consciously use them in our writing or speaking. An easy way to help us organize all the information is to develop a mind map of cry-related words and expressions, by categorizing them so as to master them. (Refer to "8.1 How to Certify (II): Mind Map" of Part I for more information) Below is a sample mind map about all the expressions related to crying found in the text and divided in categories.

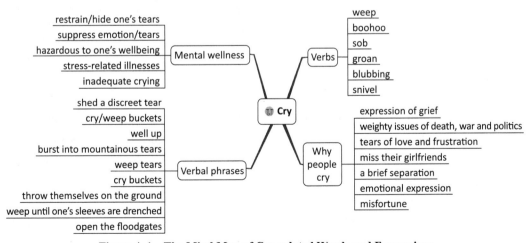

Figure 4–1   The Mind Map of Cry-related Words and Expressions

With the mind map, we have completed a comprehensive glossary on the topic. To take a further step, we can also take down some famous quotes on crying to expand our knowledge on the topic to get ourselves prepared for making strong arguments in writings and speeches. Take a look at the following quotes and see if they can be of any help to support our arguments.

- To weep is to make less the depth of grief.

    —William Shakespeare

- Excessive sorrow laughs. Excessive joy weeps.

    —William Blake

- Do not apologize for crying. Without this emotion, we are only robots.

    —Elizabeth Gilbert

- Heavy hearts, like heavy clouds in the sky, are best relieved by the letting of a little water.

    —Antoine Rivarol

- Heaven knows we need never be ashamed of our tears, for they are rain upon the blinding dust of earth, overlying our hard hearts.

    —Charles Dickens

- Tearless grief bleeds inwardly.

    —Christian Nevell Bovee

Section II

In this section, we are going to look at the essay introduction, thesis statement, and supporting details to see what techniques the author adopts to develop a fair and balanced structure.

In "4.2 and 4.3 Introductions and Conclusions (I) (II)" of Part I, various ways to begin an essay are discussed. An introduction of an essay has several roles to play: to catch readers' attention, set the background for discussion, and propose the thesis statement. The first two paragraphs of *Text A* are the introduction of the whole essay. Below is a detailed analysis of each part of the introduction.

Lead-in

One of our **most firmly entrenched ideas** of masculinity is that men don't cry. Although he might shed a discreet tear at a funeral, and it's acceptable for him to well up when he slams his fingers in a car door, a real man is expected to quickly regain control. **Sobbing openly is strictly for girls.**

Analysis: The essay title "Man, Weeping" is rather eye-catching simply, because it doesn't fit the social norm that men don't usually cry or weep. It makes perfect sense when the author begins the essay with a popular social norm, "our most firmly entrenched idea" that "men don't cry". The lead-in part of the introduction ends with a popular misconception that "Sobbing openly is strictly for girls", which does a great job in grabbing readers' attention.

Supporting Details

Analysis: The topic sentence of the second paragraph is the first line, "This isn't just a social expectation; it's a scientific fact." To support the claim of "a scientific fact", the author quotes findings from a meta-study in 2009 and presents statistics about how often and how long men and women cry respectively. The author then raises her doubt and proposes a claim that "the gender gap in crying seems to be a recent development".

Thesis Statement

Analysis: In essay writing, it is essential to present the thesis statement, loud and clear, in the introduction. "In fact, male weeping was regarded as normal in almost every part of the world for most of recorded history" at the end of the second paragraph serves as the thesis statement of the essay. It tells the author's major argument that male crying was considered normal, and narrows the scope of discussion to "most of recorded history".

Effective Expression: A Rhetorical Dimension ＼＼＼

In *Text A*, the author explores an interesting topic of men crying. She presents stories from literary works, accounts from chronicles, and scientific findings to support her argument that man's crying has long been considered normal in history, rather than shameful or feminine. In the last paragraph, she calls for greater tolerance for both men's and women's crying. To end the discussion on a rather weighty topic of crying, the author ends her essay on a light note, mainly because of some figures of speech she employs in the last paragraph.

In "5.1 A Brief Introduction to Rhetoric and Rhetorical Devices" of Part I, semantic and syntactical rhetorical devices are discussed briefly, including metaphor, hyperbole, antithesis, and pun. Let's take a closer look at the figures of speech and how they fit in the context.

First, the author begins the last paragraph with "It's time to open the floodgates". Literally, floodgate refers to the device used to control the flow of water from a large lake or river. In the context, to "open the floodgates" is used metaphorically to indicate the process of crying after suppressing emotions for a while.

Second, the author appeals to both men and women to cry when something bad happens, until "our sleeves are drenched". It is common sense that no one can actually cry for so long

and so hard that their sleeves become soaking drenched. The figure of speech used here is called "hyperbole". It is a rhetorical device that creates heightened effect through deliberate exaggeration, and one that is used to add emphasis without the intention of being literally true. Hyperbole is a common figure of speech used often in everyday writings and speeches. For example:

- She is as blind as a bat.
- The suitcase weighs a ton. What did you put in?
- Red Bull gives you wings. (Red Bull commercial advertisement)

Hyperbole is also a very common literary device. Some best-known examples of hyperbole in literature are listed as follows:

- A day was twenty-four hours long but seemed longer. There was no hurry, for there was **nowhere to go, nothing to buy** and **no money to buy it with, nothing to see** outside the boundaries of Maycomb County.

  —Harper Lee, *To Kill a Mockingbird*
- The skin on her face was as thin and drawn **as tight as the skin of onion** and her eyes were gray and **sharp like the points of two picks**.

  —Flannery O'Connor, *Parker's Back*
- At that time Bogota was a remote, lugubrious city where an **insomniac rain had been falling since the beginning of the 16th century**.

  —Gabriel García Márquez, *Living to Tell the Tale*

Third, the author ends the essay with a famous quote from the Bible, "They that sow in tears shall reap in joy." In "6.3 Parallelism and Antithesis" of Part I, a special type of parallelism is introduced—antithesis. It is a rhetorical device in which two opposite or contrasting ideas are put together in adjacent phrases, clauses, or sentences to achieve a contrasting effect. It emphasizes the idea of contrast by parallel structures. "Sow" and "reap" and "tears" and "joy" are the two pairs of contrasting ideas and are put together to deliver a more vivid and emphatic message to the readers.

Last, we may have noticed, at this point, a pun in "They that sow in tears shall reap in joy". The word "tears" indicates both hard work and the action of crying. Usually, when people make the reference in the quote, tears refer to due labor or effort necessarily required to achieve a goal. But in the context, the author makes the popular reference and incorporates the literal meaning of tears to make the end memorable.

Effective Expression: A Logical Dimension \\\\

In *Text A*, the author makes a strong argument that men shedding tears should not be regarded shameful or feminine. To support an argument, we need to look for and organize accurate, relevant, typical, and sufficient evidence, as mentioned in "7.4 How to Certify (I): Evidence" of Part I. However, evidence doesn't work alone, it has to go with some explanation of reasons, i.e. the process of reasoning. Reasoning is to organize the evidence we've found and connect it to the claim we want to make. Reasoning works like a bridge that helps to link evidence to the claim. It is the logical connection.

In "8.2, 8.3, and 8.4 How to Claim: Logic (I) (II) (III)" of Part I, we discuss common types of reasoning, which are adopted in *Text A*. Let us discuss in detail how the author connects evidence to the argument.

First, use inductive reasoning. Induction is the process of reasoning from specific facts or occurrences to general principles, theories, and rules. The author makes an argument in the second paragraph, "In fact, male weeping was regarded as normal in almost every part of the world for most of recorded history." Below is a list of all the historical evidence she includes in her argumentation.

Sources	Who Cried?
Homer, *Iliad*	• the entire army • King Priam • Zeus • the immortal horses of Achilles
Chronicles of Middle Ages	• one ambassador • the entire audience at a peace congress
The Tale of Heike	• men cited as the ideal behaviour of a samurai
Medieval romances	• knights
Chretien de Troyes, *The Knight of the Cart*	• Lancelot (twice)

Based on the evidence collected from different works in various periods of recorded history, the author makes a strong argument that "Male weeping was regarded as normal in almost every part of the world". She moves from specific facts and occurrences to arrive at a general theory. Inductive reasoning helps us to generalize from known cases to unknown principles and theories.

Second, use deductive reasoning. In the latter half of the essay, the author discusses possible causes of the disappearance of male tears. One possible reason is that in the process of urbanization from the 18th to the 20th century, people had to live with the fact that they were living with thousands of strangers, as opposed to with dozens of friends and family before the Romantic period. She quotes from *Crying: The Natural and Cultural History of Tears*, which says factory managers deliberately "trained their workers to suppress emotion". Thus, the author makes the claim that men at the time worked in factories with strangers around and learned to refrain from expressing emotions. Deductive reasoning begins with a major premise—factory managers—in this case, followed by a minor premise which is a specific example—men who worked in factories. The conclusion is therefore guaranteed.

Third, use causal reasoning. In discussing harms of men refraining from crying to their wellbeing, the author quotes three studies that intend to analyze effects of lack of crying on people. The first study establishes the relationship between inadequate crying and stress-related illnesses. The second looks at connection of people reporting higher levels of satisfaction with the amount they cry. The third study examines people who are physiologically unable to cry and their difficulty in identifying their own emotions. All the scientists in the studies reason by establishing the relationship between causes and effects. Again, through inductive reasoning, the author bases her general claim on the specific research findings.

Interactive Writing

Read *Text A* carefully and comment on the topic of male tears in NO LESS THAN 150 words.

- How come men are often seen crying in circumstances such as competitive sports? Can men only shed tears of joy? Or is it because it happens in a masculine setting?

- How do stereotypes of masculinity affect mental health of both genders?

You can support yourself with information from the text and/or include any relevant examples from your own knowledge or experience.

You should pay attention to the relevance and sufficiency of the content, organization and language quality.

_____

_____

_____

_____

★ Text B
Born to Be Different?

I grew up with *Ms.* magazine and the National Organization of Women and a firm belief that gender differences were *learned*, not inborn. Other parents may have believed that pink and baby dolls and kindergarten teaching were for girls, and blue and trucks and engineering were for boys, but my kids were going to be different. They were going to be raised free of all that harmful gender indoctrination. They were just going to be *people*.

Over the years, however, I had to rethink my earlier assumptions. Despite my best efforts not to impose gender-specific expectations on them, my boys and my girl were, well, different. Really different. Slowly and hesitantly, medical and psychological researchers have begun confirming my observations. The notion that the differences between the sexes (beyond the obvious anatomical ones) are biologically based is fraught with controversy. Such beliefs can easily be misinterpreted and used as the basis for harmful, oppressive stereotypes. They can be overstated and exaggerated into blanket statements about what men and women "can" and "can't" do; about what the genders are "good" and "bad" at. And yet, the unavoidable fact is that studies are making it ever clearer that, as groups, men and women differ in almost every measurable aspect. Learning about those differences helps us understand why men and women are simultaneously so attracted and fascinated, and yet so frequently stymied and frustrated, by the opposite sex. Our differences are deep-rooted, hard-wired, and present from the moment of conception.

To begin with, let's look at something as basic as the anatomy of the brain. Typically, men have larger skulls and brains than women. But the sexes score equally well on intelligence tests. This apparent contradiction is explained by the fact that our brains are apportioned differently. Women have about 15 percent more "gray matter" than men. Gray matter, made up of nerve cells and the branches that connect them, allows the quick transference of thought from one part of the brain to another. This high concentration of gray matter helps explain women's ability to look at many sides of an argument at once, and to do several tasks (or hold several conversations) simultaneously. Men's brains, on the other hand, have a more generous portion of "white matter". White matter, which is made up of neurons, actually inhibits the spread of information. It allows men to concentrate very narrowly on a specific task, without being distracted by thoughts that might conflict with the job at hand.

Our brains' very different makeup leads to our very different methods of interacting with the world around us. Simon Baron-Cohen, author of *The Essential Difference: Men, Women and the Extreme Male Brain*, has labeled the classic female mental process as "empathizing".

He defines empathizing as "the drive to identify another person's emotions and thoughts, and to respond to these with an appropriate emotion." Empathizers are constantly measuring and responding to the surrounding emotional temperature. They are concerned about showing sensitivity to the people around them. This empathetic quality can be observed in virtually all aspects of women's lives: from the choice of typically female-dominated careers (nursing, elementary school teaching, social work) to reading matter popular mainly with women (romantic fiction, articles about relationships, advice columns about how people can get along better) to women's interaction with one another (which typically involves intimate discussion of relationships with friends and family, and sympathy for each other's concerns). So powerful is the empathizing mindset that it even affects how the typical female memory works. Ask a woman when a particular event happened, and she often pinpoints it in terms of an occurrence that has emotional content: "That was the summer my sister broke her leg" or "That was around the time Gene and Mary got into such an awful argument." Likewise, she is likely to bring her empathetic mind to bear on geography. She'll remember a particular address not as 11th and Market Streets but being "near the restaurant where we went on our anniversary", or "around the corner from Liz's old apartment".

In contrast, Baron-Cohen calls the typical male mindset "systemizing", which he defines as "the drive to analyze and explore a system, to extract underlying rules that govern the behavior of a system". A systemizer is less interested in how people feel than in how things work. Again, the systematic brain influences virtually all aspects of the typical man's life. Male-dominated professions (such as engineering, computer programming, auto repair, and mathematics) rely heavily on systems, formulas, and patterns, and very little on the ability to intuit another person's thoughts or emotions. Reading material most popular with men includes science fiction and history, as well as factual "how-to" magazines on such topics as computers, photography, home repair, and woodworking. When they get together with male friends, men are far less likely to engage in intimate conversation than they are to share an activity: watching or playing sports, working on a car, bowling, golfing, or fishing. Men's conversation is peppered with dates and addresses, illustrating their comfort with systems: "Back in 1996 when I was living in Boston…" or "The best way to the new stadium is to go all the way out Walnut Street to 33rd and then get on the bypass…"

One final way that men and women differ is in their typical responses to problem-solving. Ironically, it may be this very activity—intended on both sides to eliminate problems— that creates the most conflict between partners of the opposite sex. To a woman, the process of solving a problem is all-important. Talking about a problem is a means of deepening the intimacy between her and her partner. The very anatomy of her brain, as well as her accompanying empathetic mindset, makes her want to consider all sides of a question and to explore various possible solutions. But men have an almost completely opposite approach when it comes to dealing with a problem. Everything in their mental makeup tells them to focus narrowly on the issue, solve it, and get it out of the way. The ability to fix a problem quickly and efficiently is, to them, a demonstration of their power and competence.

The challenge that confronts men and women is to put aside ideas of "better" and "worse" when it comes to their many differences. Our diverse brain development, our ways of interacting with the world, and our modes of dealing with problems all have their strong points. Under some circumstances, a typically feminine approach may be more effective; in others, a classically masculine mode may have the advantage. Our differences aren't going to disappear: my daughter, now a middle-schooler, regularly tells me she loves me, while her teenage brothers express their affection by grabbing me in a headlock. Learning to understand and appreciate one another's gender-specific qualities is the key to more rich and rewarding lives together.

[Source: Langan, J. 2014. *College Writing Skills with Readings* (9th ed.). Beijing: Foreign
　　　　Language Teaching and Research Press.]

Effective Expression in Practice

1. For each word or phrase in the left column, find a synonym or phrase of similar meaning from *Text B* and put them in the right column. (See "1.1 Significance of Learning Wording and Phrasing" and "1.2 Lexical Diversity" of Part I)

Words or Phrases	Synonyms or Phrases of Similar Meaning
firm belief	
overstate	
difference	
transference	
empathize	
be fraught with	
solve (a problem)	
approach	

2. In an essay that emphasizes comparison and contrast, either a point-by-point or side-by-side pattern is adopted. (See "3.2 Comparison and Contrast" of Part I for detailed discussions.) Identify which pattern is used in the following paragraphs and fill in the table.

Paragraphs	Development Patterns	Outlines
3		Thesis: Women: Men:
4 & 5		Thesis: Women: Men:
6		Thesis: Women: Men:

3. As we discussed in "3.4 Thesis Statement" of Part I, a thesis statement summarizes the major argument of the whole essay. The thesis statement of the text appears at the end of the second paragraph. We have also learned in "4.3 Introductions and Conclusions (II)" of Part I, a skillful writer tends to include an essay map in the introduction so that the readers know in advance where they're headed. The essay map gives readers a brief yet specific idea about where the essay is going so that they will never get lost. Add an essay map that follows the thesis statement.

Our differences are deep-rooted, hard-wired, and present from the moment of conception.

_____

_____

4. Various rhetorical devices are discussed in Unit 5 and Unit 6 of Part I. Find at least one example of the following devices from *Text A* or *Text B*.

Alliteration   *Example:*

_____

_____

Parallelism   *Example:*

_____

_____

Antithesis   *Example:*

_____

_____

5. In "8.2, 8.3, and 8.4 How to Claim: Logic (I) (II) (III)" of Part I, we discuss some major types of reasoning—inductive reason, deductive reasoning, and causal reasoning. Read the following claims from *Text B*, determine the types of reasoning adopted and analyze how the evidence supports the claims.

Claims	Types of Reasoning	Analyses
Men's brains and women's brains are anatomically different.		
Men and women interact with the world differently.		
Men and women have different problem-solving approaches.		

Critical Thinking in Practice

Read the following excerpt and comment on the reasons why women are underrepresented in STEM fields in NO LESS THAN 150 words. You should give specific reasons and evidence to support your argument, including examples, research, logic, or knowledge from your own experience.

Girls and Boys Are Equally Good at Math, and Children's Brains Function Similarly Regardless of Gender

Between 2015 and 2016, women made up only 35.5 percent of STEM students in the US, 32.6 percent of masters courses, and 33.7 percent at PhD level. Scientists have debunked the idea that women are underrepresented in the technology, engineering, and mathematics (STEM) industries because of biological differences which affect their math skills.

Girls and boys have similar brains and are equally able when it comes to understanding math, according to the study published in the journal *NPJ Science of Learning*. The research involved 104 children aged between 3 to 10 years old, 55 of whom were girls. The kids watched an educational video featuring maths concepts such as counting and addition, while the scientists charted their brain activity using an MRI scanner. According to the data, there was no difference between the children's brain functions or development. And the boys and girls appeared to be equally tuned into the videos. The team also looked at the results of a maths ability test taken by 97 children aged between 3 and 8 years old, 50 of whom were girls. Both genders performed equally well, regardless of age.

Unit 5   Celebrities

★ Text A

The Woman Behind the Wizard

When the final battle was over and the last secrets of the seven-book, 17-year journey were spilled, J.K. Rowling did what grieving, grateful and emotionally exhausted people do: she ransacked the minibar.

She'd known from the start that Harry Potter would survive his ordeal; the question was how she would handle her own. She had been holed up on deadline in the Balmoral Hotel in Edinburgh, Scotland, to escape the bedlam at home, writing the climactic chapter in which her hero walks into the dark forest to give his life for those he loves. And though she knew that all would be well in the end, "I really was walking him to his death, because I was about to finish writing about him," she says. It's her favorite chapter in her favorite book—but when she finished, "I just burst into tears and couldn't stop crying. I opened up the minibar and drank down one of those pathetic little bottles of champagne."

Rowling calls her time with Harry "one of the longest relationships of my adult life", her rock through bereavement, a turbulent marriage and divorce, single motherhood, changes of country, fear of failure—and transcendent joy, on the day a wise man at Bloomsbury offered her $2,250 and agreed to print 1,000 books. Fast-forward through the life of Harry. In 2007, *Harry Potter and the Deathly Hallows*, the seventh and final book in the series, sold 15 million copies worldwide in the first 24 hours it was on sale, breaking the record that had been set successively by each of the previous three books. (To put that in perspective, Book Six, 2005's *Half-Blood Prince*, moved more copies in its first day—9 million—than *The Da Vinci Code* did in its first year.) Meanwhile, the movie version of Book Five, *Order of the Phoenix*, made $645 million, and plans for the Orlando, Fla., theme park were unveiled. *Forbes* magazine put Rowling second only to Oprah as the richest woman in entertainment, and as the first person to become a billionaire by writing books.

The writer's journey that began in 1990 ended in 2007, leaving Rowling a little more margin to savor ballet recitals and grocery shopping and intensive, often ingenious charitable

work. A woman of high energy and a short fuse, she looked almost serene when we met for this piece, nearly a year after she'd finished the last book in the series. She was dressed in black with a long, gray belted sweater, dark red nails and a funky black ring the size of a walnut. But as we sat and talked over coffee, you could hear the longing when the conversation shifted back to Hogwarts, as though we'd retreated to a safe place but couldn't stay there long. "I can only say, and many of my more militant fans will find this almost impossible to believe," she says, "but I don't think anyone has mourned more than I have. It's left the most enormous gaping hole in my life."

She's funny, self-mocking and earnest by turns, but always unguarded and unrehearsed, especially since now, after all this time, she can talk about the things she had to keep secret because her readers did not want their pleasure spoiled by knowing how things would turn out. "It's a massive, massive sense of release," she says, to be able to answer any question, tell the backstory with obsessive fans who want to know the middle names of characters down to the third generation. She doesn't actually need to talk to Barbara Walters, because her fans know where to find her: her website, which includes news, a diary, a rubbish bin for addressing the more idiotic rumors, and answers to both the frequently and the never asked questions.

Parents may need to let go of their children, but artists want eternal ownership, and you can feel her ambivalence at the prospect of legions of writers who want to take up Harry's story as their own. One declared at the previous summer's biggest Potterfest that, since Rowling had left the sandbox, it was open for all to play in. "He's still mine," she says. "Many people may feel that they own him. But he's a very real character to me, and no one's thought about him more than I have."

He is also a billion-dollar media property and a global cultural figure. Now translated into 79 languages, the books have joined a canon that stretches from *Cinderella* to *Star Wars*, giving people a way to discuss culture and commerce, politics and values. Princeton English professor William Gleason compares the series' influence to the frenzy that surrounded *Uncle Tom's Cabin* before the Civil War. "That book penetrated all levels of society," he says. "It's remarkable how similar the two moments are." And he does not see this as a passing fad or some triumph of clever marketing. "They've spoken profoundly to enough readers that they will be read and reread by children and by adults for a long time," he says. Feminist scholars write papers on Hermione's road to self-determination. Law professors cite Dobby's tale to teach contract law and civil rights. University of Tennessee law professor Benjamin Barton published "Harry Potter and the Half-Crazed Bureaucracy" in the *Michigan Law Review*, which examined Rowling's view of the legitimacy of government. His conclusion? "Rowling may do more for libertarianism than anyone since John Stuart Mill."

And that is on top of the impact, even her critics acknowledge, of inspiring a generation of obsessive readers unafraid of fat books and complex plots. "They're easy to underestimate because of what I call the three Deathly Hallows for academics," says James Thomas, a professor of English at Pepperdine University. "They couldn't possibly be good because they're too recent, they're too popular, and they're too juvenile." But he argues that the books do more than entertain. "They've made millions of kids smarter, more sensitive, certainly more literate, and probably more ethical and aware of hypocrisy and lust for power. They've made children better adults, I think. I don't know of any books that have worked that kind of magic on so many millions of readers in so short a time in the history of publications."

It was the end of a long January day when the last page of the last chapter was complete. "There have been times since finishing, weak moments," she said, "when I've said, 'Yeah, all right,' to the eighth novel." But she is convinced that she's doing the right thing to take some time. "If, and it's a big if, I ever write an eighth book about the [wizarding] world, I doubt that Harry would be the central character," she says. "I feel like I've already told his story. But these are big ifs. Let's give it 10 years and see how we feel then." It's a pretty safe bet how her audience will feel. But we'll just have to wait and prepare to be surprised.

Effective Expression: A Linguistic Dimension

1. "2.4 Syntactic Variety" of Part I illustrates how to diversify the language at the sentence level. Two major methods are introduced: vary sentence length and structure, and vary sentence beginnings. In this section, a third method will also be introduced: place adjectives or verbs in a series. If those words have the same kind of structure, parallelism is created. *Text A* abounds in diversified sentences. Let's take a close look at the typical examples and analysis.

The Original Sentences	Syntactic Varieties	Analyses
She had been holed up on deadline in the Balmoral Hotel in Edinburgh, Scotland, to escape the bedlam at home, **writing** the climactic chapter in which her hero walks into the dark forest to give his life for those he loves.	vary sentence length and structure	As is explained in "2.4 Syntactic Variety" of Part I, "the first useful way is to vary sentence length and structure." Flexible use of "-ing" participles is definitely helpful for varying the sentences. In the example, "writing" is used to present supplemented information, so that the sentences don't follow the same pattern.
In 2007, *Harry Potter and the Deathly Hallows*, the seventh and final book in the series, sold 15 million copies worldwide in the first 24 hours it was on sale, **breaking** the record that had been set successively by each of the previous three books.		The paragraph, from which this example sentence is quoted, starts with a simple sentence. Right after the first sentence, this example sentence is also a simple sentence, but its structure is varied by the use of the participle "breaking". Therefore, sentence styles are diversified in this paragraph.
The writer's journey that began in 1990 ended in 2007, **leaving** Rowling a little more margin to savor ballet recitals and grocery shopping and intensive, often ingenious charitable work.		This "-ing" participle "leaving" is used to present supplemented information, and the sentence style is also varied.

(cont.)

The Original Sentences	Syntactic Varieties	Analyses
Now translated into 79 languages, the books have joined a canon that stretches from *Cinderella* to *Star Wars*, **giving** people a way to discuss culture and commerce, politics and values.	vary sentence beginnings or begin with a special opening word or phrase	Common special opening words or phrases are -ed words, -ing words, -ly words, infinitives, and prepositional phrases. In this sentence, "translated" is an -ed word, and it is used at the beginning to vary the sentence style. (See "2.4 Syntactic Variety" of Part I) This "-ing" participle "giving" is used to present supplemented information, and the sentence style is also varied.
A woman of high energy and a short fuse, she looked almost serene when we met for this piece, nearly a year after she'd finished the last book in the series.		This sentence starts with "A woman of high energy and a short fuse", which is in apposition to "she". By starting with this noun phrase, this sentence avoids repetition of the simple sentence pattern.
… J.K. Rowling did what **grieving, grateful** and **emotionally exhausted** people do…	place adjectives or verbs in a series	In this sentence, descriptive adjectives like "grieving" "grateful" and "exhausted" are presented in a series. Therefore, the sentence style is diversified.
She's **funny**, **self-mocking** and **earnest** by turns…		Expressions like "funny" "self-mocking" and "earnest" are presented in a series. With the omission of "she's" for the latter two, the sentence style is diversified.
They couldn't possibly be good **because they're too recent, they're too popular, and they're too juvenile**.	parallelism	The series of "they're too recent" "they're too popular" and "they're too juvenile" follow the similar structure, and the repetition of this structure creates parallelism. Hence, the sentence is easier to read, and the sentence style is also varied.

2. "3.2 Comparison and Contrast" of Part I illustrates how to develop a paragraph with comparison and contrast. In *Text A*, you will find out how they are used effectively.

The Original Sentences	Comparison & Contrast	Analyses
Princeton English professor William Gleason compares the series' influence to the frenzy that surrounded *Uncle Tom's Cabin* before the Civil War. "That book penetrated all levels of society," he says. "It's remarkable how similar the two moments are." And he does not see this as a passing fad or some triumph of clever marketing. "They've spoken profoundly to enough readers that they will be read and reread by children and by adults for a long time," he says.	comparison	Comparison is an effective way to develop paragraphs. It highlights similarities between two things. Although this is not the typical "point-by-point pattern" or "side-by-side pattern" (See "3.2 Comparison and Contrast" of Part I), these sentences show more details about how popular and enduring the *Harry Potter* series are. The author compares the series with *Uncle Tom's Cabin* which is a masterpiece in the world literature. Two similarities are presented in the paragraph: (1) Both works are widely accepted as in "That book penetrated all levels of society"; (2) Both works are enduring as "they will be read and reread by children and by adults for a long time". Thus, the readers will have a better understanding of the charm and legend of the *Harry Potter* series as it enjoys a wide range of audience for a long time. To sum up, comparison is an effective way to develop paragraphs and essays.
To put that in perspective, Book Six, 2005's **Half-Blood Prince**, moved **more copies in its first day—9 million—than *The Da Vinci Code* did in its first year**.	contrast	Contrast is used to develop the idea in this sentence. As is mentioned in the above analysis, we compare to find out similarities, and we contrast to find out the differences. *The Da Vinci Code* is a 2003 mystery thriller novel, and it was once the No.1 worldwide bestseller. The difference here is about the copies sold. In its first day, 2005's *Half-Blood Prince* sold more copies than the bestseller *The Da Vinci Code* did in its first year. This contrast presents the staggering fact that Book Six not only brought in greater success of the *Harry Potter* series but also built up to the magic power of Rowling. With this contrast of sold copies, readers can imagine how powerful Rowling's magic is.

(cont.)

The Original Sentences	Comparison & Contrast	Analyses
Forbes magazine put **Rowling** second only to **Oprah** as the richest woman in entertainment, and as the first person to become a billionaire by writing books.	comparison	A successful American television personality, Oprah Winfrey is the richest woman in entertainment. Put second only to Oprah by *Forbes* magazine, Rowling became a billionaire by writing books. With this focused comparison, the readers can get amazed by the success of Rowling.
"**Rowling** may do more for libertarianism than anyone since **John Stuart Mill**."		John Stuart Mill, an English philosopher, is one of the most influential thinkers in the history of classical liberalism. By comparing Rowling with John Stuart Mill, the author suggests the far-reaching influence of Rowling and her *Harry Potter* series. Besides, this is also a quotation which makes a strong argument. (See the following analysis of "quotations")

3. "4.1 Supporting Details" of Part I illustrates how to support the thesis statement with supporting details. A variety of supporting details are employed in *Text A* to support the main point. Among those various supporting details, "quotation" is a dominant feature.

The Original Sentences	Types of Supporting Details	Analyses
"That book penetrated all levels of society," he says. "It's remarkable how similar the two moments are."	quotation	The first sentence in the paragraph where the example sentence is quoted is the topic sentence. The author quotes from several sources to support it. This example sentence is also a quotation. The pronoun "he" in this example refers to William Gleason, an English professor from Princeton. By saying "all levels of society" and "remarkable", this Ivy League professor spoke highly of Rowling and her works. Therefore, this quotation from this authoritative source establishes the fact that Harry Potter is also "a billion-dollar media property and a global cultural figure". Besides, when quoting, you should also pay attention to the use of quotation marks and other punctuations.

(cont.)

The Original Sentences	Types of Supporting Details	Analyses
"They've spoken profoundly to enough readers that they will be read and reread by children and by adults for a long time," he says.	quotation	This quotation makes a strong argument for the topic sentence, and helps to explain why Harry Potter becomes "a billion-dollar media property and a global cultural figure".
"They've made millions of kids smarter, more sensitive, certainly more literate, and probably more ethical and aware of hypocrisy and lust for power. They've made children better adults, I think. I don't know of any books that have worked that kind of magic on so many millions of readers in so short a time in the history of publications."		As you can read from *Text A*, these sentences are quoted form a professor of English at Pepperdine University. This quotation is also from an authoritative source, and helps to explain the success of Rowling.

4. Signal words are also called transitional words. They are just like the glue to hold the ideas together. The "1.4 Signal Words" of Part I elaborates on five major types of signal words (emphasis words, addition words, contrast words, illustration words, and cause and effect words). While you can identify different types of signal words in *Text A*, one more method is used by the author to connect the evidence, i.e. using the same grammatical structure in several sentences to establish coherence. Let's look at the following examples and analysis.

The Original Paragraph	Method of Connecting the Evidence	Analysis
Princeton English professor William Gleason compares the series's influence to the frenzy that surrounded *Uncle Tom's Cabin* before the Civil War. "That book penetrated all levels of society," he says. "It's remarkable how similar the two moments are." And he does not see this as a passing fad or some triumph of clever marketing. "They've spoken profoundly to enough readers that they will be read and reread by children and by adults for a long time," he says. **Feminist scholars write** papers on Hermione's road to self-determination. **Law professors cite** Dobby's tale to teach contract law and civil rights. **University of Tennessee law professor Benjamin Barton published** "Harry Potter and the Half-Crazed Bureaucracy," in the *Michigan Law Review*, which examined Rowling's view of the legitimacy of government. His conclusion? "Rowling may do more for libertarianism than anyone since John Stuart Mill."	using the same grammatical structure	In writing, we use quotations as supporting evidence to support the point. When we quote from more than one source, we will also have to organize and connect the evidence. Signal words are very helpful to establish coherence. (See "1.4 Signal Words" of Part I) However, in this paragraph, the author doesn't use any signal word to connect the four examples. Instead, the author uses the same grammatical structure to establish coherence. All these examples follow the "subject plus verb" pattern, like "Princeton English professor William Gleason compares" "Feminist scholars write" "Law professors cite", and "University of Tennessee law professor Benjamin Barton published". The repeated use of the same grammatical structure creates coherence, and serves as a kind of map for the readers to follow.

Effective Expression: A Rhetorical Dimension ⟩⟩⟩

Proper use of rhetorical devices can add both power and color to your language. Vividness and persuasiveness are enhanced in *Text A* by the frequent use of metaphor and other rhetorical devices.

The Original Sentences	The Rhetorical Devices	Analyses
When the final **battle** was over and the last secrets of the seven-book, 17-year **journey** were spilled…	metaphor	In this sentence, the word "battle" is not a war, but a long-time effort of writing the *Harry Potter* series. It is not any ordinary effort, but a 17-year exclusive devotion on seven books. The metaphor used here emphasizes the hard work of Rowling. Besides, the word "journey" also embodies the hard work with the use of metaphor. The metaphoric use of "battle" and "journey" makes the language vivid and effective. (See "5.4 Metaphor" of Part I)
A woman of high energy and **a short fuse**, she looked almost serene when we met for this piece, nearly a year after she'd finished the last book in the series.		A dictionary meaning of "fuse" is "a long piece of string or paper which is lit to make a bomb or a firework explode." In this example, it is used figuratively. The author employs metaphor to compare the personality of Rowling to "a short fuse"—emotional, quite contrary to the impression of being "almost serene". Metaphor empowers the language and leaves deep impression on the readers.
One declared at the previous summer's biggest Potterfest that, since Rowling had left the **sandbox**, it was open for all to play in.		In this example, "left the sandbox" is used to state the fact that Rowling had finished writing the *Harry Potter* series. Here "sandbox" is compared to the legitimacy of writing Happy Potter series. With the use of metaphor, the language is vivid and concise.
J.K. Rowling did what grieving, grateful and emotionally exhausted people do: she **ransacked** the minibar.	hyperbole	Hyperbole is a common figure of speech. It is usually used to achieve emphasis, especially by exaggeration. According to *Oxford Dictionary*, the meaning of "ransack" is "to make a place untidy, causing damage, because you are looking for something". In the example, it is exaggerating to say that Rowling "ransacked the minibar", but the readers can imagine how she felt after finishing the series—a mixed feeling of "grieving, grateful and emotionally exhausted".
"I just burst into tears and couldn't stop crying. I opened up the minibar and drank down one of those **pathetic** little bottles of champagne."	transferred epithet	The word "pathetic" is usually used to describe people. In this example, the epithet is transferred from a person to "champagne". As little bottles of champagne were pathetic, together with other phrases like "burst into tears" and "crying", Rowling depicted vividly how she felt after finishing the series. Readers will definitely resonate with her when reading these lines.

Effective Expression: A Logical Dimension ⟩⟩⟩

In "7.4 How to Certify (I): Evidence" of Part I, the ARTS rule of choosing the evidence is introduced. Let's examine how this rule is applied and what evidence is chosen to support the argument in the text.

The Initial Letters	The Features of the Evidence	Evidence from the Text	Analyses
A	Accurate	1. … on the day a wise man at Bloomsbury offered her $2,250 and agreed to print 1,000 books. Fast-forward through the life of Harry. 2. In 2007 *Harry Potter and the Deathly Hallows*, the seventh and final book in the series, sold 15 million copies worldwide in the first 24 hours it was on sale, breaking the record that had been set successively by each of the previous three books. 3. To put that in perspective, Book Six, 2005's *Half-Blood Prince*, moved more copies in its first day—9 million—than *The Da Vinci Code* did in its first year. 4. Meanwhile, the movie version of Book Five, *Order of the Phoenix*, made $645 million… 5. The writer's journey that began in 1990 ended in 2007, leaving Rowling a little more margin to savor ballet recitals and grocery shopping and intensive, often ingenious charitable work.	Statistics always make up the accuracy and credibility of the evidence. Exact numbers and times are gathered in the text to prove the magic of J. K. Rowling. Take numbers in Example 1 as illustration. "$2,250" is not a grand amount of money, and "1,000" books can hardly be associated with any bestseller. With this humble start, Rowling persisted in her writing, and created the wizard world enchanting readers all over the world. The narration becomes dramatic with the exact numbers. The stunning numbers, "15 million" in Example 2, "9 million" in Example 3 and "$645 million" in Example 4 confirm, in an objective way, how popular the series are. In Example 5, "in 1990" and "in 2007" speak for themselves, unveiling the long-time 17-year journey Rowling had been on.
R	Relevant	See all the sentences listed in this table.	A variety of supporting details, like quotation, statistics, and explanatory examples, are employed in *Text A* to support the main point.

(cont.)

The Initial Letters	The Features of the Evidence	Evidence from the Text	Analyses
T	Typical	1. Princeton English professor William Gleason compares the series' influence to the frenzy that surrounded *Uncle Tom's Cabin* before the Civil War… 2. Feminist scholars write papers on Hermione's road to self-determination. 3. Law professors cite Dobby's tale to teach contract law and civil rights. 4. University of Tennessee law professor Benjamin Barton published "Harry Potter and the Half-Crazed Bureaucracy" in the *Michigan Law Review*…	These examples are quotations from authoritative sources, e.g. from university professors or feminist scholars. They are typical examples to support the idea that Harry Potter is "a billion-dollar media property and a global cultural figure". In Example 1 and Example 4, the author also points out the names of the university professors, making the supporting evidence persuasive.
S	Sufficient	The above examples and quotations in the linguistic dimension are some of the sufficient evidence in this article.	The author presents sufficient examples to illustrate the magic of Rowling.

Interactive Writing ＼＼＼

Read *Text A* carefully and comment on a book that has inspired you in NO LESS THAN 150 words.

You can support yourself with information from the text and/or include any relevant examples from your own knowledge or experience.

You should pay attention to the relevance and sufficiency of the content, organization and language quality.

_____

_____

_____

_____

_____

Ode to Beethoven

When we think of history's most venerated figures—scientists, political leaders, painters or musicians—our idea of them is often so overpowered by the enormity of their achievement and legacy, that we forget they were humans just like us, with their own failings and weaknesses. Ludwig van Beethoven, one of the greatest composers who ever lived, was no exception.

It was the genius mind that brought us such monumental music treasures as the rapturous "Ode to Joy" which we adopted as the European Anthem, the delicate jewellery-box sounds of "Für Elise"; and the distinctive, blood-curdling four opening notes of the Fifth Symphony. This genius mind though, belonged to a man whose psyche and life were rife with contradiction and tragedy. Childhood trauma, alcoholism, loneliness, self-doubt and an artistically crippling deafness were just a few of the issues Beethoven battled with throughout his life. Yet, as it often happens, the anguish he suffered fed and aided his creativity. Every movement, chord and note conceived by him oozes with raw suffering, despair in the face of life's unfairness and existential dread. It penetrates and digs deep into the soul, revealing to us the core of what makes us human and—inevitably—what we all share in common, ensuring his music will keep speaking to and bewitching generations to come.

Deafness

Beethoven had lost 60 percent of his hearing by 1801 when he was just 31. For someone whose entire life was centred around music, the tragedy of these circumstances must have been insurmountable. Though doctors initially told him that it would cure itself, deep down Beethoven already knew it never would.

That same year, he wrote his last will, known today as the Heiligenstadt Testament. In it he announced in utter despair, "If I do reach the stage where I can't compose anymore, and I can't hear my own music, there's no point in living." As it turned out, not only did the composer live till the age of 56 but he also wrote some of his heftiest, most ground-breaking work while completely deaf, including "Missa Solemnis" and the Ninth Symphony. He never quite abandoned his hope of hearing something, though. In 1818, he ordered a Broadwood piano from London as it was the loudest existing instrument. And while it's unlikely he could hear it play, he could probably feel the instrument's vibrations. Some of his compositions illustrate this desperate attempt in a vividly heart-breaking way. Says Scottish pianist Steven Osborne: "There is one bit in the penultimate piano sonata, where he starts repeating this note

over and over again, which gets louder and louder, until he's almost hammering it. It's a very short passage, but it is reminiscent of Beethoven banging the key just to hear something."

Wolfgang Amadeus Mozart

Mozart was an undeniable influence on Beethoven's work. In fact, when the composer moved out of his native Bonn to Vienna in 1786, he was hoping to study with Mozart, though the details of their relationship, including whether they ever actually met, remain uncertain. When Mozart died in 1791, everyone expected the talented young Beethoven to fill his shoes, and the impressionable composer initially succumbed to that pressure, styling his works so they'd have a distinct Mozartean flavour. Yet once he eventually found his own voice, the two geniuses' visions turned out to be polar opposites. American pianist Jonathan Biss says, "I always compare him with Mozart because they were almost contemporaries but they couldn't be more different. Mozart was more of an observer of human emotion and Beethoven would actually feel it, like it was a life or death matter. Listening to Beethoven you get the impression that he would set compositional problems up for himself to solve."

The Nephew

An event that profoundly hurt Beethoven was his relationship with his nephew, Karl van Beethoven. The only child of the three Beethoven brothers, he was seen by his uncle as the only chance of continuing the family's music legacy for the next generation. Feeling responsible for the boy, Beethoven tried his upmost to "rescue" him from the clutches of his sister-in-law whom he perceived as "immoral". He pushed matters to the extreme when he took Karl's mother to court to gain full custody of the child, a battle which he ended up winning but which also resulted in a painful and disappointing relationship with Karl plagued with suicide attempt sand running away from home, which devastated Beethoven creatively.

Ode to Joy

The liberating, awe-inspiring sounds of the "Ode to Joy" are arguably Beethoven's most well-known and best-loved. This monumental symphony was created when the composer was completely deaf and in his early fifties, and gave life to one of the most iconic, frequently-told stories about Beethoven: when he conducted the world premiere in Vienna in 1824, aged 54, the audience erupted in a wild applause. Since he couldn't hear, he just stood there with his back to them, prompting a soloist to turn him around so that he could see what a great triumph the piece was.

A Grouchy Genius

An eccentric his entire life, Beethoven was not one for pleasantries and social norms. Among his prime moments of societal ineptitude was waking up in the middle of the night and banging on his walls as he beat time to his music, waking up all his neighbours; or refusing to perform at soirees when he would be called upon to do so. Says John Suchet, the host of Classic FM's flagship morning show, "He was a difficult, irascible, temperamental, short, stocky man who was not easy to get on with. He has very few close friends and he managed to alienate even them. On one occasion dressed in a ragged coat tied up with string, he went for a walk at night and stared through people's windows, and he was arrested as a tramp, was taken to the police station and put behind bars."

Influence on Subsequent Music

He gripped the public's imagination a couple of centuries ago and he hasn't let go since. "His influence was crippling," says Jonathan Biss. "The personality was too big to try to replicate. Also, he took these forms, like the piano sonata or the string quartet and he pushed them beyond logical limits. There was not much left to do with them. Maybe Beethoven's greatest influence was that he forced anyone who came after to him to look in the completely opposite directions."

German composer Johannes Brahms was one of the people who felt the pressure of writing new music post-Beethoven directly. When he was in his early twenties, he was commonly regarded as the heir to Beethoven's legacy and he nearly collapsed under the weight of that comparison, saying, "You don't know what it means to the likes of us when we hear his footsteps behind us."

These footsteps continued echoing beyond the Romantic era, however, and shaped and influenced every aspect of music as we know it today, percolating even into such unexpected genres as disco or metal music and hence, redirecting new generations of listeners towards his own oeuvre. "I have no idea how we'll be consuming music in 15 years' time but I'm sure Beethoven will have a firm place in it," says Jonathan.

(Source: Mackevic, E. 2020, February 4. Ode to Beethoven. *Reader's Digest.*)

Effective Expression in Practice \\\

1. *Text B* abounds in a wide range of distinctive expressions. These unique words or phrases exhibit the importance of lexical diversity. (See "1.2 Lexical Diversity" of Part I) The following exercise will help you identify those expressions, and learn to use them in writing.

In this exercise, there are sentences or expressions with fifteen blanks. For each blank, you are required to select one word from a list of choices given in the word bank. Read the passage through carefully before making your choices. Each choice in the bank is identified by a letter. You may not use any of the words in the bank more than once. You may refer to the tips in the brackets after each sentence.

a. delicate	b. battled	c. contradiction	d. distinctive	e. anguish
f. monumental	g. gripped	h. ground-breaking	i. abandoned	j. perceived
k. wild	l. bewitching	m. undeniable	n. profoundly	o. desperate

1) He _____ the public's imagination a couple of centuries ago. (to get; to grasp)

2) His was the genius mind that brought us such _____ musical treasures as the rapturous "Ode to Joy". (important; great)

3) The _____ he suffered fed and aided his creativity. (severe pain; suffering)

4) There are the _____ jewelry-box sounds. (light and pleasant)

5) There are the _____ blood-curdling four opening notes. (different and easily noticed)

6) This genius mind though, belonged to a man whose psyche and life were rife with _____ and tragedy. (a lack of agreement)

7) Childhood trauma, alcoholism, loneliness, self-doubt and artistically crippling deafness were just a few of the issues Beethoven _____ with throughout his life. (to struggle; to fight)

8) As it turned out, not only did the composer live till the age of 56 but he also wrote some of his heftiest, most _____ work while completely deaf. (making new discoveries; using new methods)

9) He never quite _____ his hope of hearing something. (to give up)

10) Some of his compositions illustrate this _____ attempt in a vividly heart-breaking way. (needing or wanting something very much)

11) Mozart was an _____ influence on Beethoven's work. (certain)

12) An event that _____ hurt Beethoven was his relationship with his nephew. (very seriously; completely)

13) Feeling responsible for the boy, Beethoven tried his utmost to "rescue" him from the clutches of his sister-in-law whom he _____ as "immoral". (to understand; to think)

14) The audience erupted in a _____ applause. (strong)

15) His music will keep speaking to and _____ generations to come. (attracting)

2. As we learned in "3.4 Thesis Statement" of Part I, an effective thesis statement is crucial to help develop a persuasive essay. Do you still remember what a thesis statement is? What are the essential parts of an effective thesis statement? What should be taken into consideration when you write a thesis statement? In the first paragraph of *Text B*, the author expresses his opinion on the subject. Can you identify the subject and the author's opinion? If you are to write a thesis statement for *Text B*, how will you write it? Think about the questions and fill in the table.

Items	Your Answers
Definition	
Two essential parts	
Considerations	
The subject of *Text B*	
The author's opinion in *Text B*	
Your thesis statement	

3. Go through *Text B*, and find out the sentences whose natural orders are changed for emphasis, and the emphatic sentences as well. Think about how the emphasis is shifted.

The "2.4 Syntactic Variety" of Part I explained linguistic diversity at the sentence level. Two suggestions are very helpful for writing or improving your language: The first useful way is to vary sentence length and structure; varying sentence beginnings is also a useful way to diversify sentences. Emphatic sentences are typical examples. Another different approach in writing diversified sentences is to change the word order, i.e. change the natural order of sentences. However, we do not change the order randomly. Order is changed for emphasis or for the balance of sentences. Negatives are typical examples. (See "2.4 Syntactic Variety" of

Part I). In *Text B*, you can also find sentences whose natural orders are changed.

Example 1: _____

Analysis: _____

Example 2: _____

Analysis: _____

Example 3: _____

Analysis: _____

4. Rhetorical devices are introduced in Unit 5 of Part I. Identify rhetorical devices in the following sentences from *Text B*.

A. … a battle which he ended up winning but which also resulted in a painful and disappointing relationship with Karl…

Rhetorical devices: _____

B. … insuring his music will keep speaking to and bewitching generations to come.

Rhetorical devices: _____

C. When Mozart died in 1791, everyone expected the talented young Beethoven to fill his shoes…

Rhetorical devices: _____

D. You don't know what it means to the likes of us when we hear his footsteps behind us.

Rhetorical devices: _____

5. In *Text B*, the author writes that "the anguish he suffered fed and aided his creativity", which is supported in different supporting paragraphs. In this paragraph about deafness, how is the rule of ARTS in choosing evidence used to support that idea (See "7.4 How to Certify (I): Evidence" of Part I)? Find out the evidence, identify its types (See "4.1 Supporting Details" of Part I), and fill in the table.

The Initial Letters	The Features of the Evidence	Examples	Types of Evidence
A	Accurate		
R	Relevant		
T	Typical		
S	Sufficient		

Critical Thinking in Practice ＼＼＼

Read the following excerpt carefully and comment on the excerpt in NO LESS THAN 150 words.

Beethoven had lost 60 percent of his hearing by 1801 when he was just 31. For someone whose entire life was centred around music, the tragedy of these circumstances must have been insurmountable. Though doctors initially told him that it would cure itself, deep down Beethoven already knew it never would. That same year, he wrote his last will, known today as the Heiligenstadt Testament. In it he announced in utter despair, "If I do reach the stage where I can't compose anymore, and I can't hear my own music, there's no point in living." As it turned out, not only did the composer live till the age of 56 but he also wrote some of his heftiest, most ground-breaking work while completely deaf, including "Missa Solemnis" and the Ninth Symphony.

Unit 6 Business

★ Text A
Co-opetition

The moon landing just over 50 years ago is remembered as the culmination of a fierce competition between the United States and the Soviet Union. But in fact, space exploration almost started with cooperation. President Kennedy proposed a joint mission to the moon when he met with Khrushchev in 1961 and again when he addressed the United Nations in 1963. It never came to pass, but in 1975 the Cold War rivals began working together on Apollo-Soyuz, and by 1998 the jointly managed International Space Station had ushered in an era of collaboration. Today a number of countries are trying to achieve a presence on the moon, and again there are calls for them to team up. Even the hypercompetitive Jeff Bezos and Elon Musk once met to discuss combining their Blue Origin and SpaceX ventures.

There is a name for the mix of competition and cooperation: co-opetition. In 1996, when we wrote a book about this phenomenon in business, instances of it were relatively rare. Now the practice is common in a wide range of industries, having been adopted by rivals such as Apple and Samsung, DHL and UPS, Ford and GM, and Google and Yahoo.

There are many reasons for competitors to cooperate. At the simplest level, it can be a way to save costs and avoid duplication of effort. If a project is too big or too risky for one company to manage, collaboration may be the only option. In other cases, one party is better at doing A while the other is better at B, and they can trade skills. And even if one party is better at A and the other has no better B to offer, it may still make sense to share A at a right price.

Co-opetition raises strategic questions, however. How will the competitive dynamics in your industry change if you cooperate—or if you don't? Will you be able to safeguard your most valuable assets? Careful analysis is required. In this article we'll provide a practical framework for thinking through the decision to cooperate with rivals.

If a cooperative opportunity is on the table, start by imagining what each party will do if it's not taken. What alternative agreements might the other side make, and what alternatives might you pursue? If you don't agree to the deal, will someone else take your place in it? In particular, will the status quo still be an option?

Let's start with a simple example. Honest Tea was approached by Safeway supermarkets to make a private-label line of organic teas. The new line would undoubtedly eat into Honest Tea's existing Safeway sales. So even though the supermarket was offering a fair price, the deal would ultimately be unprofitable for Honest Tea.

However, if Honest Tea didn't cooperate, Safeway would surely find another supplier, such as rival tea maker Tazo. Honest figured that if it took the deal, it could design the new Safeway "O Organics" line to resemble the flavors and sweetness of Tazo's products and compete less against its own. If Honest had said no, Tazo would probably have said yes and targeted Honest's flavors, leading to the worst possible outcome. So Honest agreed to the deal.

Yet the company turned down a similar request from Whole Foods because the grocery chain insisted that the private line include a clone of Moroccan Mint, Honest's best-selling tea at the time. Honest didn't want to compete so directly against itself and believed that its rivals would have trouble copying the tea—which indeed turned out to be true.

UPS had to think through a similar opportunity when DHL, which had acquired Airborne Express some years earlier and was suffering large losses, asked UPS to fly DHL's packages within the United States. UPS had the scale to make the service efficient (potentially saving DHL $1 billion a year) and was already providing a similar service to the US Postal Service, so the opportunity appeared to be a profitable one that would allow UPS to rent out space on planes it was already flying.

That said, not cooperating might have been even more profitable in the long run. If DHL's continuing losses led to its exit, UPS stood to gain much of DHL's US market share. But if UPS turned the deal down, DHL might have offered it to FedEx. And if FedEx accepted it, DHL would still be in the market and UPS would have lost out on potential profits. So UPS agreed to DHL's proposal, announcing a deal in May, 2008. (It turned out to be not enough to save DHL, which decided during the recession later that year to leave the market.)

In the tech industry, thinking through alternatives to a deal is complicated because companies have multiple relationships with one another. Samsung's decision about whether to sell Apple its new Super Retina edge-to-edge OLED screen for the iPhone X is a good example.

Samsung could have temporarily hurt Apple in the high-end smartphone market—where the Samsung Galaxy and iPhone compete—by not supplying its industry-leading screen. But Apple isn't the only rival Samsung has to worry about. In addition to being one of the world's largest phone manufacturers, Samsung is also one of the largest suppliers to phone manufacturers (including Apple, across several generations). If it hadn't provided its Super

Retina display to Apple, Apple could have turned to LG (which supplies OLED screens for Google's Pixel 3 phones) or BOE (which supplies AMOLED screens for Huawei's Mate 20 Pro phones), strengthening one of Samsung's screen-technology competitors. Plus, Apple is well-known for helping its suppliers improve their quality. Cooperating with Apple meant that Samsung would get this benefit and that its screen-technology rivals would not. The fact that the deal would increase Samsung's scale and came with a big check attached—an estimated $110 for each iPhone X sold—ultimately tilted the balance toward cooperating.

It takes two to cooperate. Now let's look at the deal from Apple's perspective. Would it make Samsung a more formidable rival? It probably would: In the year prior to the iPhone X launch, revenue from Apple accounted for almost 30% of the Samsung display business, a division that generated $5 billion in profits. (Apple was also buying DRAM and NAND flash memory chips, batteries, ceramics, and radio-frequency-printed circuit boards from Samsung.) But for Apple, getting the best screen was worth bankrolling an already well-resourced rival—at least for a while.

The underlying economic reason that working together was advantageous to both sides was that Samsung had the best screen and Apple had a loyal customer base. Without cooperating, neither company could get the extra value from putting the superior screen on the new iPhone.

We began this article with the missed opportunity for cooperation between the United States and the Soviet Union on a mission to the moon. Today the opportunities for countries to cooperate are even larger—from tackling COVID-19 and climate change to resolving trade wars. We hope that a better understanding of co-opetition will help businesses, managers, and countries find a better way to work and succeed together.

(Source: Brandenburger, A. & Nalebuff, B. 2021, January 1. Co-opetition. *Harvard Business Review*.)

Effective Expression: A Linguistic Dimension ﹨﹨﹨

1. The "4.2 Introductions and Conclusions (I)" and "4.3 Introductions and Conclusions (II)" of Part I illustrate effective ways to write introductions and conclusions. Make a close analysis at the introduction and conclusion in *Text A*.

The Original Sentences	Ways to Write Introductions / Conclusions	Analyses
President Kennedy proposed a joint mission to the moon when he met with Khrushchev in 1961 and again when he addressed the United Nations in 1963. It never came to pass, but in 1975 the Cold War rivals began working together on Apollo-Soyuz, and by 1998 the jointly managed International Space Station had ushered in an era of collaboration.	anecdote	An anecdote can be a short personal account of an incident or event; or it can also be a story that you tell people about something interesting or funny that has happened to you. In *Text A*, the author tells a story about the unexpected and unprecedented collaboration between two rival superpowers—the United States and the Soviet Union. This anecdote serves as a lead-in for the whole article, and it undoubtedly grabs the readers' attention. It is a successful example of attention-grabber for lead-in in the introductory paragraph. (See "4.2 Introductions and Conclusions (I)" of Part I)
We began this article with the missed opportunity for cooperation between the United States and the Soviet Union on a mission to the moon. Today the opportunities for countries to cooperate are even larger—from tackling COVID-19 and climate change to resolving trade wars. We hope that a better understanding of co-opetition will help businesses, managers, and countries find a better way to work and succeed together.	final thought	In conclusion, you don't simply make a word-to-word copy of the thesis statement (See "3.4 Thesis Statement" of Part I). Try to paraphrase it and reemphasize the author's opinion. (See "4.3 Introductions and Conclusions (II)" of Part I) Here are some common ways to bring your essay to a natural end, such as: a. an end with a summary and final thought b. an end with a thought-provoking quotation c. an end with a prediction d. an end with a recommendation When writing a conclusion, you may use one or a combination of methods to round off your essay. The conclusion of *Text A* presents a final thought of the topic "co-opetition", and it invites the readers to reflect upon it in different situations and times.

2. The "4.1 Supporting Details" of Part I illustrates how to support the thesis statement with supporting details. A variety of supporting details are employed in *Text A* to support the main point, such as anecdotes, statistics, definitions, reason analysis, etc. Make a close analysis at supporting details in *Text A*.

The Original Sentences	Types of Supporting Details	Analyses
There is a name for the mix of competition and cooperation: co-opetition. In 1996, when we wrote a book about this phenomenon in business, instances of it were relatively rare. Now the practice is common in a wide range of industries, having been adopted by rivals such as Apple and Samsung, DHL and UPS, Ford and GM, and Google and Yahoo.	definition	Before you present supporting evidence, you may sometimes need to define one or two key terms so that the discussion is focused and manageable. (See "4.1 Supporting Details" of Part I) In the very first paragraph, the author defines the new term "co-opetition" so that the following discussion is manageable. Besides, the readers are also appealed by this new term, and will find no obstacle in understating the following arguments. The purpose here in *Text A* is to explain a new business term "co-opetition". The author mainly uses two strategies to explain the new term: (1) word formation; (2) stating some examples. With word-formation, the sentence — "There is a name for the mix of competition and cooperation" — illustrates how the new term "co-opetition" came into being: the prefix "co" of "cooperation" plus "o" from "cooperation" and "petition" from "competition". With the analysis of word-formation, readers will easily get the meaning of the newly coined term "co-opetition", which means the collaboration between competitors. The examples of Apple and Samsung, DHL and UPS, Ford and GM, and Google and Yahoo present typical examples about the new term "co-opetition". The strategy of stating some examples is used, and therefore, the readers can have a better understanding of this new term.

(cont.)

The Original Sentences	Types of Supporting Details	Analyses
There are many reasons for competitors to cooperate. **At the simplest level**, it can be a way to save costs and avoid duplication of effort. If a project is too big or too risky for one company to manage, collaboration may be the only option. **In other cases**, one party is better at doing A while the other is better at B, and they can trade skills. **And even** if one party is better at A and the other has no better B to offer, it may still make sense to share A at the right price.	reason analysis	Reason analysis is also necessary in argumentative writing. Instead of directly jumping to supporting evidence, you can actually make a more complete and stronger case by analyzing reasons. This is all about the whole argumentation process. (See "4.1 Supporting Details" of Part I) Additionally, when you analyze more than one reason, you will have to connect the reasons with transitional words. (See "4.4 Body Paragraphs" of Part I) In this paragraph, the author analyzes three reasons for co-opetition, which are connected by transitional words to achieve coherence. These transitional words are "at the simplest level" "In other cases", and "And even". With flexible use of the transitional words, the author explains one by one why competitors need to cooperate.
The fact that the deal would increase Samsung's scale and came with a big check attached—an estimated **$110** for each iPhone X sold—ultimately tilted the balance toward cooperating.	statistics	Statistics are usually persuasive. In this sentence, "$110" proves the importance of cooperation between rivals. (See "4.1 Supporting Details" of Part I)
It probably would: In the year prior to the iPhone X launch, revenue from Apple accounted for almost **30%** of the Samsung display business, a division that generated $5 billion in profits.		Statistics like "30%" and "$5 billion" are used here to support the point. (See "4.1 Supporting Details" of Part I)

(cont.)

The Original Sentences	Types of Supporting Details	Analyses
Let's start with a simple example. **Honest Tea** (which one of us cofounded) was approached by Safeway supermarkets to make a private-label line of organic teas. The new line would undoubtedly eat into Honest Tea's existing Safeway sales. So even though the supermarket was offering a fair price, the deal would ultimately be unprofitable for Honest Tea. However, if **Honest Tea** didn't cooperate, Safeway would surely find another supplier, such as rival tea maker Tazo. Honest figured that if it took the deal, it could design the new Safeway "O Organics" line to resemble the flavors and sweetness of Tazo's products and compete less against its own. If Honest had said no, Tazo would probably have said yes and targeted Honest's flavors, leading to the worst possible outcome. So Honest agreed to the deal.	explanatory examples	In essay writing, explanatory examples are also called "exemplification". The verb "exemplify" means: (1) to be a typical example of something; (2) to give an example in order to make something clearer. Explanatory examples help your audience fully understand your point. Lively, specific examples also add color to your writing. *Text A* presents plentiful of examples to make the point clear, i.e. to explain what "co-opetition" is, and how it operates in business. This example of Honest Tea explains how rivals work together to generate profits—a typical example of "co-opetition". Therefore, the readers can understand in depth the new term "co-opetition", its importance, and how it works in business.
UPS had to think through a similar opportunity when **DHL**, which had acquired Airborne Express some years earlier and was suffering large losses, asked UPS to fly DHL's packages within the United States. UPS had the scale to make the service efficient (potentially saving DHL $1 billion a year) and was already providing a similar service to the US Postal Service, so the opportunity appeared to be a profitable one that would allow UPS to rent out space on planes it was already flying.		In this paragraph, the author explains how UPS thought through the risks and rewards to work with its rival DHL. This example serves as supporting details to further illustrate the concept of "co-opetition", and how it works in business. In the following paragraphs, when explaining the "co-opetition" between Samsung and Apple, the author also employs examples to exemplify.

(cont.)

The Original Sentences	Types of Supporting Details	Analyses
What Is Likely to Happen If You Don't Cooperate? …	causal analysis	Causal analysis is another important method to develop your essay. (See "8.4 How to Claim: Logic (III)" of Part I)

Some essays of causal analysis focus primarily on the cause(s) of something; others mainly analyze the effect(s); still others discuss both causes and effects. To make it simple, cause asks: Why does "X" happen? Effect asks: What does "Y" produce?

In *Text A*, the author mainly focuses on the effects. He follows this model: What does "Y" produce? Here "Y" refers to the decision whether Honest Tea should cooperate with its rivals.

Then the author writes two separate paragraphs to discuss two possible consequences, i.e. what would happen if Honest Tea cooperated with its rivals or what else would happen if it would not. With causal analysis, the author offers elaborate and convincing supporting details. |

Effective Expression: A Rhetorical Dimension

Proper use of rhetorical devices can add both power and color to your language. Vividness and persuasiveness are enhanced in *Text A* by the use of metonymy and metaphor.

The Original Sentences	The Rhetorical Devices	Analyses
In other cases, one party is better at doing **A** while the other is better at **B**, and they can trade skills. And even if one party is better at **A** and the other has no better **B** to offer, it may still make sense to share A at the right price.	metonymy	Metonymy is a very useful rhetorical device. It substitutes one thing for another, and compress much information into a simple word or phrase. In the example, "A" might be a business plan, a project, a press conference for new products, etc., while "B" means those different from "A". All the possibilities cannot be exhausted, but "A" or "B" can be used to substitute those different situations. Therefore, the use of metonymy contributes to the conciseness of the language.

(cont.)

The Original Sentences	The Rhetorical Devices	Analyses
If a cooperative opportunity is **on the table**, start by imagining what each party will do if it's *not* taken.	metonymy	In this example, "the table" does not mean the dinner table, but a situation in which an offer, a plan, a proposal or something else is under discussion for cooperative opportunity, similar to an object that is physically placed on a table. The phrase "on the table" can be seen as a metonymy because it is used to represent the cooperative opportunity or proposal under discussion. The use of metonymy makes the language vivid.
1. However, if **Honest Tea** didn't cooperate, **Safeway** would surely find another supplier, such as rival tea maker **Tazo**. 2. **UPS** had to think through a similar opportunity when **DHL**, which had acquired **Airborne Express** some years earlier and was suffering large losses, asked **UPS** to fly **DHL**'s packages within the United States. 3. **Samsung** could have temporarily hurt **Apple** in the high-end smartphone market—where the Samsung Galaxy and iPhone compete— by not supplying its industry-leading screen.		In Example 1, "Honest Tea" is associated with the company that produces tea with the brand of "Honest Tea". The author uses "Honest Tea" to substitute the company, so that the language is brief. This method is also employed for "Safeway" and "Tazo". By substituting the companies with their products, the author embodies the language with conciseness. What's more, *Text A* also becomes more reader-friendly as the readers will not be confused by the repetitive use of such words as "company". To sum up, with the use of metonymy, the language is concise and intelligible. In Example 2, you can also easily identify the use of metonymy. "UPS" "DHL" and "Airborne Express" are all used to substitute the companies which are associated with those brands. In Example 3, you can also find substitute words, like "Samsung" "Apple", etc. (See "6.1 Metonymy and Synecdoche" of Part I)

Effective Expression: A Logical Dimension

Various supporting evidence for co-opetition is forcefully demonstrated in *Text A*. In "7.4 How to Certify (I): Evidence", the ARTS rule of choosing the evidence is introduced. Let's examine how this rule is applied and what evidence is chosen to support the argument in the text.

The Initial Letters	The Features of the Evidence	Evidence from the Text	Analyses
A	Accurate	1. President Kennedy proposed a joint mission to the moon when he met with Khrushchev in **1961** and again when he addressed the United Nations in **1963**. It never came to pass, but in **1975** the Cold War rivals began working together on Apollo-Soyuz, and by **1998** the jointly managed International Space Station had ushered in an era of collaboration.	Statistics always make up the accuracy and credibility of the evidence. Exact numbers, times and ratio are gathered in the text to prove co-opetition is beneficial for rival competitors. Thus the key viewpoint is backed up forcefully.
		2. UPS had the scale to make the service efficient (potentially saving DHL **$1 billion** a year) and was already providing a similar service to the US.	In Example 1, the anecdote becomes credible with accurate presentation of the timeline starting in 1961 and ending in 1998.
		3. The fact that the deal would increase Samsung's scale and came with a big check attached—an estimated **$110** for each iPhone X sold—ultimately tilted the balance toward cooperating.	In Examples 2, 3 & 4, the readers will realize the importance of co-opetition with staggering numbers, like "$1 billion a year" "$110" "30%" and "$5 billion". These numbers contribute to the credibility of supporting details.
		4. It probably would: In the year prior to the iPhone X launch, revenue from Apple accounted for almost **30%** of the Samsung display business, a division that generated **$5 billion** in profits.	
R	Relevant	See those example sentences listed in the above two dimensions.	A variety of supporting details, like definition, reason analysis, statistics, explanatory examples, causal analysis, are employed in *Text A* to support the main point.

(cont.)

The Initial Letters	The Features of the Evidence	Evidence from the Text	Analyses
T	Typical	1. **The moon landing** just over 50 years ago is remembered as the culmination of a fierce competition between the **United States** and the **Soviet Union**. But in fact, space exploration almost started with cooperation. 2. Even the hypercompetitive **Jeff Bezos** and **Elon Musk** once met to discuss combining their **Blue Origin** and **SpaceX** ventures. 3. **Honest Tea** (which one of us cofounded) was approached by **Safeway supermarkets** to make a private-label line of organic teas. 4. **UPS** had to think through a similar opportunity when **DHL**, which had acquired Airborne Express some years earlier and was suffering large losses, asked **UPS** to fly **DHL**'s packages within the United States. 5. **Samsung** could have temporarily hurt **Apple** in the high-end smartphone market—where the **Samsung Galaxy** and **iPhone** compete—by not supplying its industry-leading screen.	When it comes to co-opetition, no example can be more typical and persuasive than the cooperation between the United States and the Soviet Union. As these two rival superpowers "ushered in an era of collaboration", the new term "co-opetition" becomes intelligible. Blue Origin and SpaceX are two private space exploration companies. Blue Origin was initiated by Jeff Bezos, who ranked No. 1 on *Forbes*' 35th annual list of the world's wealthiest in 2021. SpaceX was initiated by Elon Musk who ranked No.2 on the same list. These companies are shaping the future of space travel, and you can imagine the fierce competition between them. When the world's richest people call for cooperation for their rivalry business, the importance of co-opetition becomes self-evident. For Examples 3, 4 & 5, you can read how rivals, like Honest Tea and Safeway, UPS and DHL, and Samsung and Apple, became partners and started cooperation. All those are house-hold names in the business world, and they serve as typical examples in *Text A*.

(cont.)

The Initial Letters	The Features of the Evidence	Evidence from the Text	Analyses
S	Sufficient	1. The moon landing just over 50 years ago is remembered as the culmination of a fierce competition between the United States and the Soviet Union… 2. Even the hypercompetitive Jeff Bezos and Elon Musk once met to discuss combining their Blue Origin and SpaceX ventures… 3. However, if Honest Tea didn't cooperate, Safeway would surely find another supplier, such as rival tea maker Tazo… 4. Yet the company turned down a similar request from Whole Foods because… 5. UPS had to think through a similar opportunity when DHL… 6. Samsung's decision about whether to sell Apple its new Super Retina edge-to-edge OLED screen for the iPhone X is a good example…	The author presents sufficient examples to illustrate the concept and importance of co-opetition. The main point of *Text A* is reinforced by those supporting examples.

Interactive Writing

Read *Text A* carefully and comment on co-opetition in NO LESS THAN 150 words.

You can support yourself with information from the text and/or include any relevant examples from your own knowledge or experience.

You should pay attention to the relevance and sufficiency of the content, organization and language quality.

_____

_____

_____

_____

_____

★ Text B
Persuading the Unpersuadable

The legend of Steve Jobs is that he transformed our lives with the strength of his convictions. The key to his greatness, the story goes, was his ability to bend the world to his vision. The reality is that much of Apple's success came from his team's pushing him to rethink his positions. If Jobs hadn't surrounded himself with people who knew how to change his mind, he might not have changed the world.

For years Jobs insisted he would never make a phone. After his team finally persuaded him to reconsider, he banned outside apps; it took another year to get him to reverse that stance. Within nine months the App Store had a billion downloads, and a decade later the iPhone had generated more than $1 trillion in revenue.

Almost every leader has studied the genius of Jobs, but surprisingly few have studied the genius of those who managed to influence him. As an organizational psychologist, I've spent time with a number of people who succeeded in motivating him to think again, and I've analyzed the science behind their techniques. The bad news is that plenty of leaders are so sure of themselves that they reject worthy opinions and ideas from others and refuse to abandon their own bad ones. The good news is that it is possible to get even the most overconfident, stubborn, narcissistic, and disagreeable people to open their minds.

A growing body of evidence shows that personality traits aren't necessarily consistent from one situation to the next. Think of the dominant manager who is occasionally submissive, the hypercompetitive colleague who sporadically becomes cooperative, or the chronic procrastinator who finishes some projects early. Every leader has an "if… then" profile: a pattern of responding to particular scenarios in certain ways. If the dominant manager is interacting with a superior… then she becomes submissive. If the competitive colleague is dealing with an important client… then he shifts into cooperative mode. If the procrastinator has a crucial deadline coming up… then she gets her act together.

Computer code is a string of "if… then" commands. Humans are a lot messier, but we too have predictable "if… then" responses. Even the most rigid people flex at times, and even the most open-minded have moments when they shut down. So if you want to reason with people who seem unreasonable, pay attention to instances when they—or others like them—change their minds. Here are some approaches that can help you encourage a know-it-all to recognize when there's something to be learned, a stubborn colleague to make a U-turn, a narcissist to show humility, and a disagreeable boss to agree with you.

The first barrier to changing someone's view is arrogance. We've all encountered leaders who are overconfident: They don't know what they don't know. If you call out their ignorance directly, they may get defensive. A better approach is to let them recognize the gaps in their own understanding.

In a series of experiments, psychologists asked Yale students to rate their knowledge of how everyday objects, such as televisions and toilets, work. The students were supremely confident in their knowledge—until they were asked to write out their explanations step-by-step. As they struggled to articulate how a TV transmits a picture and a toilet flushes, their overconfidence melted away. They suddenly realized how little they understood.

Trying to explain something complex can be a humbling experience—even for someone like Steve Jobs.

A few years ago I met Wendell Weeks, the CEO of Corning, which makes the glass for the iPhone. That relationship began when Jobs reached out to him, frustrated that the plastic face of the iPhone prototype kept getting scratched. Jobs wanted strong glass to cover the display, but his team at Apple had sampled some of Corning's glass and found it too fragile. Weeks explained that he could think of three ways to develop something better. "I don't know that I'd make the glass for you," he told Jobs, "but I'd be very happy to talk with any members of your team who are technical enough to talk this thing through." Jobs responded, "I'm technical enough!"

When Weeks flew out to Cupertino, Jobs tried to tell him how to make the glass. Instead of arguing, Weeks let him explain the way his preferred method would work. As Jobs started talking, it became clear to both of them that he didn't fully understand how to design glass that wouldn't shatter. That was the opening Weeks needed. He walked to a whiteboard and said, "Let me teach you some science, and then we can have a great conversation." Jobs agreed, and Weeks eventually sketched out the glass composition, complete with molecules and sodium and potassium ion exchanges. They ended up doing it Weeks' way. The day the iPhone launched, Weeks received a message from Jobs that's now framed in his office: "We couldn't have done it without you."

(Source: Grant, A. 2021, March 1. Persuading the unpersuadable. *Harvard Business Review.*)

Effective Expression in Practice

1. *Text B* features words or expressions used to describe people. Some of them express totally different meanings. Find out the expressions which express the opposite meaning, and write them down. (See "1.2 Lexical Diversity" of Part I)

A. _____

B. _____

C. _____

2. A variety of supporting details are employed in *Text B* to support the main point. Try to find out those supporting details and identify their types. (See "4.1 Supporting Details" of Part I)

Example 1: _____

Types of Supporting Details: _____

Example 2: _____

Types of Supporting Details: _____

Example 3: _____

Types of Supporting Details: _____

3. Decide what rhetorical devices are used in the following sentences.

A. Computer code is a string of "if... then" commands. Humans are a lot messier, but we too have predictable "if... then" responses.
   Rhetorical devices: _____

B. Every leader has an "if... then" profile: a pattern of responding to particular scenarios in certain ways.
   Rhetorical devices: _____

C. As they struggled to articulate how a TV transmits a picture and a toilet flushes, their overconfidence melted away.
   Rhetorical devices: _____

4. How is the rule of ARTS in choosing evidence used in this text? Find out the evidence and fill in the table (See "7.4 How to Certify (I): Evidence" of Part I).

The Initial Letters	The Features of the Evidence	Evidence from the Text
A	Accurate	
R	Relevant	
T	Typical	
S	Sufficient	

Critical Thinking in Practice

Read the following excerpt carefully and comment on the excerpt in NO LESS THAN 150 words.

Computer code is a string of "if... then" commands. Humans are a lot messier, but we too have predictable "if... then" responses. Even the most rigid people flex at times, and even the most open-minded have moments when they shut down. So if you want to reason with people who seem unreasonable, pay attention to instances when they—or others like them—change their minds. Here are some approaches that can help you encourage a know-it-all to recognize when there's something to be learned, a stubborn colleague to make a U-turn, a narcissist to show humility, and a disagreeable boss to agree with you.

Unit 7 Science and Technology

Reading in a Whole New Way

As technology improves, how does the act of reading change?

Reading and writing, like all technologies, are constantly changing. In ancient times, authors often dictated their books. Dictation sounded like an uninterrupted series of words, so scribes wrote these down in one long continuous string, just as they occur in speech. For this reason, text was written without spaces between words until the 11th century.

This continuous script made books hard to read, so only a few people were accomplished at reading them aloud to others. Being able to read silently to yourself was considered an amazing talent; writing was an even rarer skill. In fact, in the 15th-century Europe, only one in 20 adult males could write.

After Gutenberg's invention of the printing press in about 1440, mass-produced books changed the way people read and wrote. The technology of printing increased the number of words available, and more types of media, such as newspapers and magazines, broadened what was written about. Authors no longer had to produce scholarly works, as was common until then, but could write, for example, inexpensive, heart-rending love stories or publish autobiographies, even if they were unknown.

In time, the power of the written word gave birth to the idea of authority and expertise. Laws were compiled into official documents; contracts were written down and nothing was valid unless it was in this form. Painting, music, architecture, dance were all important, but the heartbeat of many cultures was the turning pages of a book. By the early 19th century, public libraries had been built in many cities.

Today, words are migrating from paper to computers, phones, laptops and game consoles. Some 4.5 billion digital screens illuminate our lives. Letters are no longer fixed in black ink on paper, but flitter on a glass surface in a rainbow of colors as fast as our eyes can blink. Screens fill our pockets, briefcases, cars, living-room walls and the sides of buildings. They sit in front of us when we work—regardless of what we do. And of course, these newly ubiquitous screens have changed how we read and write.

The first screens that overtook culture, several decades ago—the big, fat, warm tubes of television—reduced the time we spent reading to such an extent that it seemed as if reading and writing were over. Educators and parents worried deeply that the TV generation would be unable to write. But the interconnected, cool, thin displays of computer screens launched an epidemic of writing that continues to swell. As a consequence, the amount of time people spend reading has almost tripled since 1980. By 2008, the World Wide Web contained more than a trillion pages, and that total grows rapidly every day.

But it is not book reading or newspaper reading, it is screen reading. Screens are always on, and, unlike books, we never stop staring at them. This new platform is very visual, and it is gradually merging words with moving images. You might think of this new medium as books we watch, or television we read. We also use screens to present data, and this encourages numeracy: visualising data and reading charts, looking at pictures and symbols are all part of this new literacy.

Screens engage our bodies, too. The most we may do while reading a book is to flip the pages or turn over a corner, but when we use a screen, we interact with what we see. In the futuristic movie *Minority Report*, the main character stands in front of a screen and hunts through huge amounts of information as if conducting an orchestra. Just as it seemed strange five centuries ago to see someone read silently, in the future it will seem strange to read without moving your body.

In addition, screens encourage more utilitarian (practical) thinking. A new idea or unfamiliar fact will cause a reflex to do something: to research a word, to question your screen "friends" for their opinions or to find alternative views. Book reading strengthened our analytical skills, encouraging us to think carefully about how we feel. Screen reading, on the other hand, encourages quick responses, associating this idea with another, equipping us to deal with the thousands of new thoughts expressed every day. For example, we review a movie for our friends while we watch it; we read the owner's manual of a device we see in a shop before we purchase it, rather than after we get home and discover that it can't do what we need it to do.

Screens provoke action instead of persuasion. Propaganda is less effective, and false information is hard to deliver in a world of screens because while misinformation travels fast, corrections do, too. On a screen, it is often easier to correct a falsehood than to tell one in the first place. Wikipedia works so well because it removes an error in a single click. In books, we find a revealed truth; on the screen, we assemble our own truth from pieces. What is more, a screen can reveal the inner nature of things. Waving the camera eye of a smart phone over the

bar code of a manufactured product reveals its price, origins and even relevant comments by other owners. It is as if the screen displays the object's intangible essence. A popular children's toy (Webkinz) instills stuffed animals with a virtual character that is 'hidden' inside; a screen enables children to play with this inner character online in a virtual world.

In the near future, screens will be the first place we'll look for answers, for friends, for news, for meaning, for our sense of who we are and who we can be.

(Source: Kelly, K. 2010, August 1. Reading in a whole new way. *Smithsonian*.)

Effective Expression: A Linguistic Dimension ＼＼＼

"3.2 Comparison and Contrast" of Part I illustrates how to develop a paragraph by way of contrast. Contrast is also frequently used at syntactic level to make the relevant ideas fully illustrated. The comparative structure, times and some fixed structure are adopted in *Text A* to depict the different features of reading at various periods to highlight the influence of technology on reading. Let's take a close look at those expressions and structures.

The Original Sentences	The Expressions or Structures	Analyses
Letters are **no longer** fixed in black ink on paper, **but** flitter on a glass surface in a rainbow of colors as fast as our eyes can blink.	**...no longer..., but...**	Differences in three aspects are presented here: Ways: fixed/flitter Colors: black / a rainbow of colors Media: paper and ink / a glass surface
1. Educators and parents worried deeply that the TV generation would be unable to write. **But** the interconnected, cool, thin displays of computer screens launched an epidemic of writing that continues to swell. 2. The most we may do while reading a book is to flip the pages or turn over a corner, **but** when we use a screen, we interact with what we see.	**...but...**	"But" is usually used as a conjunction for transition to show the difference or contrast. The first sentence presents the sharp contrast between the real situation and the worries of the educators and parents. The second sentence discloses the obvious difference between book reading and screen reading.
As a consequence, the amount of time people spend reading **has** almost **tripled** since 1980.	**triple**	Multiples can show the relations between the two sides directly. Here are two more frequently used ones: double: to increase twofold quadruple: to increase fourfold
On a screen, it is often **easier** to correct a falsehood **than** to tell one in the first place.	**easier... than**	The comparative structure is often used to compare two persons or things with regard to the amount of a particular quality they possess. It is also used to show two different aspects of the same person or thing. For example: He is more bold than brave.

(cont.)

The Original Sentences	The Expressions or Structures	Analyses
But it is not book reading or newspaper reading, **it is** screen reading.	**but it is not... it is...**	This structure also takes the following form: It is not... but... For example: It is not who is right but what is right that is of importance.
Book reading strengthened our analytical skills, encouraging us to think carefully about how we feel. Screen reading, **on the other hand**, encourages quick responses, associating this idea with another, equipping us to deal with the thousands of new thoughts expressed every day	**... on the other hand...**	Usually, "on the other hand" is used together with "on one hand" to list two different aspects of a certain thing. Here "on one hand" is omitted in the first sentence, which describes the feature of book reading. Both book reading and screen reading are ways of reading, just two different types.
We read the owner's manual of a device we see in a shop before we purchase it, **rather than** after we get home and discover that it can't do what we need it to do.	**... rather than...**	Here are some more examples: He is rather an explorer than a sailor. I would rather stay at home than go there. I would stay at home rather than go there. This discussion aimed at solution rather than the emotion.
Screens provoke action **instead of** persuasion.	**... instead of...**	Pay attention to the difference between "instead of" and "instead". For example: The Internet does not break us apart, but brings us closer instead. Instead of breaking us apart, the Internet brings us closer.
In books, we find a revealed truth; on the screen, we assemble our own truth from pieces.	**;**	Semicolon is also an effective way to show contrast. It can directly combine two independent sentences together.

Effective Expression: A Rhetorical Dimension

Proper use of rhetorical devices can add both power and color to your language. Vividness and persuasiveness are enhanced in *Text A* by the use of simile, metaphor and analogy, etc.

Comparison in a broad sense is also effective in showing the similarity. All such expressions and structures featuring comparison are listed as follows:

The Original Sentences	The Expressions or Structures	Analyses
Reading and writing, **like** all technologies, are constantly changing.	**A like B**	The subject of this sentence is "Reading and writing", with the preposition "like" introducing "all technologies", to show the similarity of "constantly changing". Since all technologies are constantly changing, there is no exception for the technology of reading. This sentence naturally ushers in the following changes of reading.
Dictation **sounded like** an uninterrupted series of words, …	**A sounds like B**	"Dictation" shares the similarity of being "uninterrupted" with "series of words", which is the very feature of it.
1. … so scribes wrote these down in one long continuous string, **just as** they occur in speech. 2. **Just as** it seemed strange five centuries ago to see someone read silently, in the future it will seem strange to read without moving your body.	**just as**	As described in Sentence One, what was written down was "in one long continuous string". Writing and speaking at that time had one thing in common: being continuous. The two forms are put together by "just as" to highlight the similarity between them. Sentence Two depicts the similarity between the way of reading silently five centuries ago and the way of reading without moving one's body in the future, namely strangeness. The two ways are compared here to echo the theme of the whole passage: The ways of reading are constantly changing.
Painting, music, architecture, dance were all important, but the **heartbeat** of many cultures was the turning pages of a book.	**A is B**	"Heartbeat" here does not literally mean "the actual beat of a person's heart", but metaphorically means "the core of something". The original sentence can be understood as "The turning pages of a book are the heartbeat of many cultures". In this sense, we can take the usage of "heartbeat" here as a metaphor in a broad sense. The importance of the book is accentuated vividly: Without books, many cultures cannot live.

(cont.)

The Original Sentences	The Expressions or Structures	Analyses
1. The first screens that overtook culture, several decades ago—the big, fat, warm tubes of television—reduced the time we spent reading to such an extent that it seemed **as if** reading and writing were over. 2. In the futuristic movie *Minority Report*, the main character stands in front of a screen and hunts through huge amounts of information **as if** conducting an orchestra. 3. It is **as if** the screen displays the object's intangible essence.	**as if**	In Sentence One, with the emergence of television, people spent less and less time reading. It seemed that reading and writing were almost going to be replaced. "As if" is used here to stress the severity. To support the topic sentence "Screens engage our bodies, too" at the beginning of this paragraph, Sentence Two presents the scenario in the futuristic movie. The main character interacts with the screen when searching for information in the same way as conducting an orchestra, which leaves the reader a strong impression of the new way of screen reading. The sentence before Sentence Three in *Text A* describes the convenience of scanning the bar code of a manufactured product to reveal all the related information about it. The screen seems to have the magic power to display the inner essence of things.

Effective Expression: A Logical Dimension ❯❯❯

Various changes brought by screen reading are forcefully demonstrated in *Text A*. In "7.4 How to Certify (I): Evidence" of Part I, the ARTS rule of choosing the evidence is introduced. Let's examine how this rule is applied and what evidence is chosen to support the argument in the text.

The Initial Letters	The Features of the Evidence	Evidence from the Text	Analyses
A	Accurate	1. Some **4.5 billion** digital screens illuminate our lives. 2. By 2008, the World Wide Web contained more than **a trillion** pages, and that total grows rapidly every day. 3. As a consequence, the amount of time people spend reading **has almost tripled** since 1980. 4. Being able to read silently to yourself was considered an amazing talent; writing was an even rarer skill. In fact, in the 15th-century Europe, only **one in 20** adult males could write.	Statistics always make up the accuracy and credibility of the evidence. Exact numbers, times and the ratio are gathered in the text to prove "changes" are obvious. Thus, the key viewpoint is backed up forcefully.
R	Relevant	See those sample sentences listed in the above two dimensions.	Contrast and comparison are both effective means to introduce the evidence related to the point under discussion. Those examples and/or aspects involved are similar, close or opposite to each other.
T	Typical	1. After **Gutenberg**'s invention of the printing press in about 1440, mass-produced books changed the way people read and wrote. 2. On a screen, it is often easier to correct a falsehood than to tell one in the first place. **Wikipedia** works so well because it removes an error in a single click. 3. The most we may do while reading a book is to flip the pages or turn over a corner, but when we use a screen, we interact with what we see. In the futuristic movie **Minority Report**, the main character stands in front of a screen and hunts through huge amounts of information as if conducting an orchestra.	Gutenberg, as a name, never ceases to be linked to mass printing in human history. As to the change of the way people read and wrote, whose name is more influential than his? In Case Two, the first sentence puts forward the author's idea that to correct a false on a screen is often easier than to tell one in the first place. The second sentence lists Wikipedia as one of the most typical examples succeeding in doing this. In order to support the statement "... but when we use a screen, we interact with what we see.", the author enumerates the futuristic movie *Minority Report* starred by Tom Cruise, a famous Hollywood superstar. Conducting-an-orchestra style of interacting with a screen is adopted as a typical evidence, which impresses the reader deeply and supports the viewpoint.

(cont.)

The Initial Letters	The Features of the Evidence	Evidence from the Text	Analyses
S	Sufficient	1. In ancient times… 2. until the 11th century… 3. in the 15th-century Europe… 4. in about 1440… 5. By the early 19th century… 6. Today, … 7. since 1980… 8. By 2008… 9. In the near future…	To answer the question at the very beginning "How does the act of reading change?", the author lists sufficient changes chronologically. The main point of the text is well supported by those evidence given on the timeline.

Interactive Writing

Read *Text A* carefully and comment on the impact of technology on reading in NO LESS THAN 150 words.

You can support yourself with information from the text and/or include any relevant examples from your own knowledge or experience.

You should pay attention to the relevance and sufficiency of the content, organization and language quality.

_____

_____

_____

_____

_____

_____

★ Text B

Is Technology Harming Our Children's Health?

Technology is moving at such a breakneck speed that it is enough to make your head spin. It can be difficult to keep up. However, with each new technological marvel come consequences. Much of the research conducted has shown the extent of the damage being done to our health by technology. It is a scary thought, and with teenagers and children being heavy consumers and users of these gadgets, they run the risk of being harmed the most.

Experts say that continuously listening to loud music on the small music players can permanently damage hear cells in the inner ear, resulting in hearing loss. For instance, old-fashioned headphones have been replaced with smaller ones that fit neatly into the ear, instead of over them, which intensifies the sound.

Apart from hearing damage, there are other serious health risks. We are living in a wireless age. Calls can be made and received on mobiles from anywhere and the internet can be accessed without the need for cables. The advantages are enormous, bringing ease and convenience to our lives. It is clear that mobiles and wireless technology are here to stay but are we paying the price for new technology? Studies have shown that the rapid expansion in the use of wireless technology has brought with it a new form of radiation.

Research shows that teenagers and young adults are the largest group of mobile phone users. According to a recent Eurobarometer survey, 70 percent of Europeans aged 12–13 own a mobile phone and the number of five-to-nine-year-old children owning mobiles has greatly increased over the years. Children are especially vulnerable because their brains and nervous systems are not as immune to attack as adults. Sir William Stewart, chairman of the National Radiological Protection Board, says there is mounting evidence to prove the harmful effects of wireless technologies and that families should monitor their children's use of them.

Besides the physical and biological damage, technology can also have serious mental implications for children. It can be the cause of severe, addictive behaviour. In one case, two children had to be admitted into a mental health clinic in Northern Spain because of their addiction to mobile phones. An average of six hours a day would be spent talking, texting and playing games on their phones. The children could not be separated from their phones and showed disturbed behaviour that was making them fail at school. They regularly deceived family members to obtain money to buy phone cards to fund their destructive habit. There have been other cases of phone addiction like this.

Technology may also be changing our brain patterns. Professor Greenfield, a top specialist in brain development, says that, thanks to technology, teenage minds are developing differently

from those of previous generations. Her main concern is over computer games. She claims that living in a virtual world where actions are rewarded without needing to think about the moral implications makes young people lose awareness of who they are. She claims that technology brings a decline in linguistic creativity.

As technology keeps moving at a rapid pace and everyone clamours for the new must-have gadget of the moment, we cannot easily perceive the long-term effects on our health. Unfortunately, it is the most vulnerable members of our society that will be affected.

(Source: Mini-ielts Editorial Team. 2023. Is technology harming our children's health? Retrieved June 1, 2023, from Mini-ielts website.)

Effective Expression in Practice \\\

1. Pick out the words or expressions from *Text B* which means "something develops quickly". (See "1.2 Lexical Diversity" of Part I)

A. _____

B. _____

C. _____

2. Identify the topic sentence of each paragraph and underline them in *Text B*. (See "3.4 Thesis Statement" of Part I)

3. How is the rule of ARTS in choosing evidence used in this text? Find out the evidence and fill in the table. (See "7.4 How to Certify (I): Evidence" of Part I)

The Features of the Evidence	Evidence from the Text
Accurate	According to a recent Eurobarometer survey, 70 percent of Europeans aged 12–13 own a mobile phone and the number of five-to-nine-year-old children owning mobiles has greatly increased.
Relevant	
Typical	
Sufficient	

4. Complete the following "Cause-Effect" pairs. (See " 8.4 How to Claim: Logic (III)" of Part I)

Causes	Effects
	permanently damage hear cells in the inner ear, resulting in hearing loss
the rapid expansion in the use of wireless technology	
	young people lose awareness of who they are

Critical Thinking in Practice \\\

Read the following excerpt carefully and comment on the topic in NO LESS THAN 150 words.

With Intelligent Machines to Do the Thinking, Will Our Brains Get Lazy?

Changing technology stimulates the brain and increases intelligence. But that may only be true if the technology challenges us. In a world run by intelligent machines, our lives could get a lot simpler. Would that make us less intelligent?

Artificial intelligence is embedded in many features of modem life for the simple reason that intelligent machines can already outperform humans, including some aptitudes where there was once thought to be a human advantage, such as playing chess, and writing poetry, or even novels. Artificial intelligence is taking over many human jobs.

As machines get smarter, they will do more of our thinking for us and make life easier. In the future, the electronic assistant will develop to the point that it serves similar functions as a real living butler. At that point, our long struggle with challenging technologies is at an end. Starved of mental effort, our brains will regress.

Unit 8 Environment

★ Text A
Three Environmental Issues and Ways to Combat Them

For years now, humans have mistreated and contaminated the very environment that sustains them. But the broad concern for the environment can be so overwhelming that people don't know what to do or where to start making a difference.

The list of issues surrounding our environment go on, but there are three major ones that affect the majority of them overall: global warming and climate change; water pollution and ocean acidification; and loss of biodiversity. These three issues need immediate attention and proactive action on our part to ensure conservation of the only habitable planet which we call our home. And, focusing attention on these three major topics will have a ripple effect on a number of smaller environmental issues like inefficient recycling systems and food waste.

Let's look at three major environmental issues and some solutions which can help combat them:

Global Warming and Climate Change

Human activities have made global warming and climate change a global threat. The rising levels of CO_2 and other greenhouse gases have caused an increase in average global temperatures, extreme weather events, rising sea levels and other negative changes. These changes are directly and indirectly affecting all life forms. Pollution of air, land and water through excessive deforestation, industrialization and overfilling landfills which emits CO_2 and adds to greenhouse gas emissions are all topmost causes of these environmental issues. Here are some effective solutions to these problems:

- Invest in and encourage production of sustainable technology

- Achieve zero-emission or zero-waste in commercial and residential buildings

- Improve waste compaction in landfills with smart technology like stationary compactors which helps free up space for other constructive uses. It comes in varying capacities and configurations for handling different volumes of trash

- Increase forest cover, restore sea grasses and boost use of agricultural cover crops to reduce the amount of CO_2 in atmosphere.

Water Pollution and Ocean Acidification

Rapid urban development, improper sewage disposal by industries, oil spills, disposal of chemical and radioactive wastes, and plastic pollution are some of the major causes of water pollution. Today, water scarcity and polluted water are posing a big threat to the human existence across many nations of the world.

Ocean waters absorb around 30 percent of the carbon dioxide that is released in the atmosphere. Ocean acidification occurs when the CO_2 absorbed by the seawater undergoes a series of chemical reactions which leads to increased concentration of hydrogen ions, thus making the seawater more acidic. This decreases the carbonate ions in the seawater which makes it difficult for clams, deep sea corals, oysters etc. to build and maintain their shells and other calcium carbonate structures. These changes in the ocean water chemistry can affect the behavior of other organisms also. This puts the entire ocean food web at risk. Listed below are some measures which can help prevent water pollution and ocean acidification:

- Practice more effective measures to contain spills
- Curtail storm water runoff and plant trees near water bodies to reduce soil erosion
- Expand the network which monitors the measuring of acidity levels to provide researchers and shellfish farmers with long-term and real-time pH data
- Incorporate ocean acidification threats into the coastal zone management plans of states
- Increase marine protection measures

Loss of Biodiversity

Biodiversity helps maintain the balance of the ecosystem and provides biological resources which are crucial for our existence. Habitat destruction, climate change, pollution, secondary extinction and introduced species are a few ways in which humans are wreaking havoc on the biodiversity of this planet. Loss of biodiversity can be countered in a number of ways:

- Create and implement stricter policies and laws related to conservation of biodiversity
- Stop habitat destruction and encourage its restoration
- Practice sustainable living

- Reduce invasive species

- Educate the populace about it

Awareness and adaption are two key steps towards conserving this boon called environment. Each one of us can and should do our bit to curb the effects of these environmental issues and ensure that our future generations have a healthy planet to live.

(Source: Lawson, E. 2019, November 25. Three environmental issues and ways to combat them. *Environmental Protection*.)

Effective Expression: A Linguistic Dimension

According to "1.2 Lexical Diversity" of Part I, the lexical diversity refers to using different expressions for the same or similar meaning, which can avoid repetition. The following are some synonyms used in the text to achieve diversity at the lexical level.

Chinese Meanings	English Synonyms
增加	add, rise, increase, expand
减少	curtail, reduce, decrease
促进	boost, encourage
污染	contaminate, pollute
保持，保护	maintain, conserve, preserve
破坏	havoc, destruction
释放	release, emit
不同的	varying, different

Effective Expression: A Rhetorical Dimension

As stated in "6.3 Parallelism and Antithesis" of Part I, parallelism is a repetition of a set of grammatical structures to show that a pair or list of ideas have equal weight or share equal importance. The whole text of *Text A* is arranged in a quite paralleled structure as its title suggested "Three Environmental Issues and Ways to Combat Them". Three subtitles on the environmental issues are three paralleled nominal phrases: Global Warming and Climate Change, Water Pollution and Ocean Acidification, and Loss of Biodiversity. Their respective countermeasures are listed in the paralleled structure in the bulletin point pattern. Thus, the logic of this text is very clear and lucid, letting all the readers know exactly what "Each one of us can and should do our bit to curb the effects of these environmental issues".

Effective Expression: A Logical Dimension

According to "8.4 How to Claim: Logic (Ⅲ)" of Part I, the relation between causes and effects is the key to support ourselves with evidence. They can be organized in the following patterns: single cause-effect relation; mutual cause-effect relation; one cause, multiple effects; one effect, multiple causes; multiple causes, multiple effects. Let's examine how causes and effects are organized to support the argument in the text.

Causes and Effects	The Cause-Effect Patterns
The rising levels of CO_2 and other greenhouse gases have caused an increase in average global temperatures, extreme weather events, rising sea levels and other negative changes. These changes are directly and indirectly affecting all life forms. Pollution of air, land and water through excessive deforestation, industrialization and overfilling landfills which emits CO_2 and adds to greenhouse gas emissions are all topmost causes of these environmental issues.	multiple causes, multiple effects
Rapid urban development, improper sewage disposal by industries, oil spills, disposal of chemical and radioactive wastes, and plastic pollution are some of the major causes of water pollution.	one effect, multiple causes
Ocean acidification occurs when the CO_2 absorbed by the seawater undergoes a series of chemical reactions which leads to increased concentration of hydrogen ions, thus making the seawater more acidic. This decreases the carbonate ions in the seawater which makes it difficult for clams, deep sea corals, oysters etc. to build and maintain their shells and other calcium carbonate structures. These changes in the ocean water chemistry can affect the behavior of other organisms also. This puts the entire ocean food web at risk.	one cause, multiple effects
Habitat destruction, climate change, pollution, secondary extinction and introduced species are a few ways in which humans are wreaking havoc on the biodiversity of this planet.	one effect, multiple causes

Interactive Writing

Read *Text A* carefully and comment on one environmental issue mentioned in the text and suggest measures to address the issue in NO LESS THAN 150 words.

You can support yourself with information from the text and/or include any relevant examples from your own knowledge or experience.

You should pay attention to the relevance and sufficiency of the content, organization and language quality.

_____

_____

_____

_____

_____

The Truth About the Environment

For many environmentalists, the world seems to be getting worse. They have developed a hit-list of our main fears: that natural resources are running out; that the population is ever growing, leaving less and less to eat; that species are becoming extinct in vast numbers, and that the planet's air and water are becoming ever more polluted.

But a quick look at the facts shows a different picture. First, energy and other natural resources have become more abundant, not less so, since the book *The Limits to Growth* was published in 1972 by a group of scientists. Second, more food is now produced per head of the world's population than at any time in history. Fewer people are starving. Third, although species are indeed becoming extinct, only about 0.7% of them are expected to disappear in the next 50 years, not 25%–50%, as has so often been predicted. And finally, most forms of environmental pollution either appear to have been exaggerated, or are transient-associated with the early phases of industrialisation and therefore best cured not by restricting economic growth, but by accelerating it. One form of pollution—the release of greenhouse gases that causes global warming—does appear to be a phenomenon that is going to extend well into our future, but its total impact is unlikely to pose a devastating problem. A bigger problem may well turn out to be an inappropriate response to it.

Yet opinion polls suggest that many people nurture the belief that environmental standards are declining and four factors seem to cause this disjunction between perception and reality.

One is the lopsidedness built into scientific research. Scientific funding goes mainly to areas with many problems. That may be wise policy, but it will also create an impression that many more potential problems exist than is the case.

Secondly, environmental groups need to be noticed by the mass media. They also need to keep the money rolling in. Understandably, perhaps, they sometimes overstate their arguments. In 1997, for example, the World Wide Fund for Nature issued a press release entitled: "Two thirds of the world's forests lost forever". The truth turns out to be nearer 20%.

Though these groups are run overwhelmingly by selfless folk, they nevertheless share many of the characteristics of other lobby groups. That would matter less if people applied the same degree of skepticism to environmental lobbying as they do to lobby groups in other fields. A trade organisation arguing for, say, weaker pollution controls is instantly seen as self-interested. Yet a green organisation opposing such a weakening is seen as altruistic, even if an impartial view of the controls in question might suggest they are doing more harm than good.

A third source of confusion is the attitude of the media. People are clearly more curious about bad news than good. Newspapers and broadcasters are there to provide what the public wants. That, however, can lead to significant distortions of perception. An example was America's encounter with El Nino in 1997 and 1998. This climatic phenomenon was accused of wrecking tourism, causing allergies, melting the ski-slopes and causing 22 deaths. However, according to an article in the Bulletin of the American Meteorological Society, the damage it did was estimated at US$4 billion but the benefits amounted to some US$19 billion. These came from higher winter temperatures (which saved an estimated 850 lives, reduced heating costs and diminished spring floods caused by meltwaters).

The fourth factor is poor individual perception. People worry that the endless rise in the amount of stuff everyone throws away will cause the world to run out of places to dispose of waste. Yet, even if America's trash output continues to rise as it has done in the past, and even if the American population doubles by 2100, all the rubbish America produces through the entire 21st century will still take up only one-12,000th of the area of the entire United States.

So what of global warming? As we know, carbon dioxide emissions are causing the planet to warm. The best estimates are that the temperatures will rise by 2–3°C in this century, causing considerable problems, at a total cost of US$5,000 billion.

Despite the intuition that something drastic needs to be done about such a costly problem, economic analyses clearly show it will be far more expensive to cut carbon dioxide emissions radically than to pay the costs of adaptation to the increased temperatures. A model by one of the main authors of the United Nations Climate Change Panel shows how an expected temperature increase of 2.1 degrees in 2100 would only be diminished to an increase of 1.9 degrees. Or to put it another way, the temperature increase that the planet would have experienced in 2094 would be postponed to 2100.

So this does not prevent global warming, but merely buys the world six years. Yet the cost of reducing carbon dioxide emissions, for the United States alone, will be higher than the cost of solving the world's single, most pressing health problem: providing universal access to clean drinking water and sanitation. Such measures would avoid 2 million deaths every year, and prevent half a billion people from becoming seriously ill.

It is crucial that we look at the facts if we want to make the best possible decisions for the future. It may be costly to be overly optimistic—but more costly still to be too pessimistic.

(Source: Mini-ielts Editorial Team. 2023. The truth about the environment. Retrieved June 1, 2023, from Mini-ielts website.)

Effective Expression in Practice

1. *Text B* begins with a list of the fears of those environmentalists. Such a beginning grabs the attention of the readers right away since those fears are prevailing among the public. Point out the type of the lead-in of *Text B* and identify the thesis statement. (See "4.2 Introductions and Conclusions (I)" of Part I)

The Lead-in Type: _____

The Thesis Statement: _____

2. The prevailing fears at the very beginning of *Text B* followed by the refutations one by one. From "4.1 Supporting Details" of Part I, you know that various types of supporting details are necessary to justify your argumentation, including authoritative references, statistics, reason analysis, etc. Fill in the following table by picking out the supporting details from the text.

The Fears of Many Environmentalists	The Facts and Analyses
…natural resources are running out…	
…the population is ever growing, leaving less and less to eat…	
…species are becoming extinct in vast numbers…	
…the planet's air and water are becoming ever more polluted…	

3. According to "5.1 A Brief Introduction to Rhetoric and Rhetorical Devices" of Part I, contrast is one of the semantic rhetorical devices. Apart from antonyms like "less/more" "harm/good" and "bad/good", there are such pairs sharp in contrast in *Text B*. Fill in the following table.

English Words	Antonyms
restrict	
self-interested	
lopsided	
optimistic	

4. From "8.3 How to Claim: Logic (II)" of Part I, you know that deductive reasoning moves from the general statement to the specific case. Fill in the following table with relevant information from the text.

General Statements	Specific Cases
Secondly, environmental groups need to be noticed by the mass media. They also need to keep the money rolling in. Understandably, perhaps, they sometimes overstate their arguments.	
People are clearly more curious about bad news than good. Newspapers and broadcasters are there to provide what the public wants. That, however, can lead to significant distortions of perception.	
Despite the intuition that something drastic needs to be done about such a costly problem, economic analyses clearly show it will be far more expensive to cut carbon dioxide emissions radically than to pay the costs of adaptation to the increased temperatures.	

Critical Thinking in Practice ＼＼＼

Read the following excerpt carefully and comment on the topic in NO LESS THAN 150 words.

Can Humans Restore the Biodiversity?

Just 3% of the world's land remains ecologically intact with healthy populations of all its original animals and undisturbed habitat, a study suggests. The researchers suggest reintroducing a small number of important species to some damaged areas, such as elephants or wolves—a move that could restore up to 20% of the world's land to ecological intactness.

Previous analyses have identified wilderness areas based largely on satellite images and estimated that 20%–40% of the earth's surface is little affected by humans. However, the scientists behind the new study argue that forests, savannah and tundra can appear intact from above but that, on the ground, vital species are missing. Elephants, for example, spread seeds and create important clearings in forests, while wolves can control populations of deer and elk.

The new assessment combines maps of human damage to habitat with maps showing where animals have disappeared from their original ranges or are too few in number to maintain a healthy ecosystem. Some scientists said the new analysis underestimates the intact areas, because the ranges of animals centuries ago are poorly known and the new maps do not

take account of the impacts of the climate crisis, which is changing the ranges of species.

It is widely accepted that the world is in a biodiversity crisis, with many wildlife populations—from lions to insects—plunging, mainly due to the destruction of habitats for farming and building. Some scientists think the sixth mass extinction of life on the earth is beginning, with serious consequences for the food, and clean water and air that humanity depends upon.

References

Adams, K. 2014. *Inside Writing: The Academic Wordlist in Context.* New York: Oxford University Press.

Bassham, G., Irwin, W., Nardone, H. & Wallace, M. J. 2011. *Critical Thinking: A Student's Introduction* (4th ed.). New York: McGraw-Hill.

Bowden, J. 1997. *Writing a Report: A Step-by-Step Guide to Effective Report Writing* (4th ed.). Oxford: How-to Books.

Brink-Budgen, R. V. D. 2011. *Advanced Critical Thinking Skills.* New York: How-to Books.

Broderick, B. 1996. *Groundwork for College Reading* (2nd ed.). Marlton: Townsend Press.

Buzan, T. 2003. *Mind Mapping: Scientific Research and Studies.* New York: ThinkBuzan.

Buzan, T. 2012. *The Ultimate Book of Mind Maps.* London: Harper Collins.

Chatfield, T. 2017. *Critical Thinking: Your Guide to Effective Argument, Successful Analysis and Independent Study.* Los Angeles: Sage.

Clark, S. & Pointon, G. 2007. *Word for Word.* New York: Oxford University Press.

Darlene, S. W. & Sue, J. 2010. *Technical Writing for Success* (3rd ed.). Mason: South-Western Cengage Learning.

Fowler, H. R. & Aaron, J. E. 2003. *The Little, Brown Handbook* (9th ed.). New York: Pearson.

Gamble, T. W. & Gamble, W. M. 2018. *The Public Speaking Playbook* (2nd ed.). Thousand Oaks: Sage.

Govier, T. 2010. *A Practical Study of Argument* (7th ed.). Boston: Wadsworth/Cengage Learning.

Hanscomb, S. 2017. *Critical Thinking: The Basics.* New York: Routledge.

Huber, B. R. & Snider, C. A. 2005. *Influencing Through Argument.* New York: International Debate Education Association.

Hyerle, N. D. & Alper, L. 2012. *Student Successes with Thinking Maps: School-Based Research, Results, and Models for Achievement Using Visual Tools* (2nd ed.). Thousand Oaks: Corwin.

Strunk, W. Jr. & White, B. E. 1999. *The Elements of Style* (4th ed.). New York: Pearson.

Kemper, D., Meyer, V. & Rys, J. V. 2016. *Fusion: Integrated Reading and Writing* (2nd ed.). Boston: Cengage Learning.

Kriszner, G. L. & Mandell, R. S. 2008. *Writing First with Reading: Practice in Context* (4th ed.). Boston: Bedford Saint Martin's.

Kuhn, D. & Udell, W. 2003. *The Development of Argument Skills.* Child Development, *74*(5): 1245–1260.

Langan, J. 2013. *Reading and Study Skills.* New York: McGraw-Hill.

Langan, J. 2014. *College Writing Skills with Readings* (9th ed.). Beijing: Foreign Language Teaching and Research Press.

Lucas, S. E. 2020. *The Art of Public Speaking*. New York: McGraw-Hill Education.

Nadell, J., Langan, J. & Comodromos, A. E. 2007. *The Longman Writer: Rhetoric, Reader, Research Guide, and Handbook* (7th ed.). New York: Longman.

Paul, R., Niewoehner, R. & Elder, L. 2016. *Thinker's Guide Library*. Beijing: Foreign Language Teaching and Research Press.

Radford, A. 2009. *An Introduction to English Sentence Structure*. New York: Oxford University Press.

Ramage, D. J., Bean, C. J. & Johnson, J. 2009. *Writing Arguments: A Rhetoric with Readings* (8th ed.). New York: Longman.

Rise, B. A. & Charles, R. C. 2011. *Axelrod and Cooper's Concise Guide to Writing* (6th ed.). New York: Bedford Books.

Rosenwasser, D. & Stephen, J. 2008. *Writing Analytically* (5th ed.). Boston: Thomson Wadsworth.

Rubens, P. 2002. *Science and Technical Writing: A Manual of Style* (2nd ed.). New York: Routledge.

Rustler, F. 2012. *Mind Mapping for Dummies*. West Sussex: John Wiley and Sons.

Savage, A. 2007. *Effective Academic Writing 1: The Paragraph*. New York: Oxford University Press.

Seale, C. 2020. *Thinking like a Lawyer: A Framework for Teaching Critical Thinking to All Students*. London: Prufrock Press.

Shea, H. R., Scanlon, L. & Aufses, D. R. 2008. *The Language of Composition: Reading, Writing, Rhetoric*. Boston: Bedford St. Martin's.

Shiach, D. 2007. *How to Write Essays: A Step-by-Step Guide for All Levels, with Sample Essays*. Oxford: How-to Books.

Swan, M. 2005. *Practical English Usage* (3rd ed.). New York: Oxford University Press.

Wallwork, A. 2014. *User Guides, Manuals, and Technical Writing: A Guide to Professional English*. New York: Springer.

White, J. 2015. *Taking Sides: Clashing Views in Gender* (6th ed.). Beijing: Foreign Language Teaching and Research Press.

Williams, M. J. & Bizup, J. 2013. *Style: Lessons in Clarity and Grace* (11th ed.). New York: Pearson Education.

Wyrick, J. 2017. *Steps to Writing Well* (10th ed.). Boston: Cengage Learning.

Zinsser, W. 2016. *On Writing Well: The Classic Guide to Writing Nonfiction*. New York: Harper Collins.

陈资璧，卢慈伟. 2012. 你的第一本思维导图操作书. 长沙：湖南人民出版社.

丁往道. 1994. 英语写作手册. 北京：外语教学与研究出版社.

冯翠华. 2005. 英语修辞大全（修订版）. 北京：外语教学与研究出版社.

胡曙中. 2020. 现代英语修辞学. 上海：上海外语教育出版社.

兰甘. 2007. 美国大学英语写作（第六版）. 北京：外语教学与研究出版社.

兰甘. 2008. 大学英语阅读进阶（第四版）. 北京：外语教学与研究出版社.

李莉文 , 孙有中 . 2016. 大学英语思辨教程写作 2：说明文写作 . 北京：外语教学与研究出版社 .

摩尔 . 2021. 批判性思维 . 北京：机械工业出版社 .

保罗 . 2019. 批判性思维与创造性思维 . 北京：外语教育与研究出版社 .

保罗 . 2020. 批判性思维工具 . 北京：机械工业出版社 .

曲智男 . 2017. 画出你的世界：思维导图实战手册 . 北京：电子工业出版社 .

石坚，帅培天 . 2010. 英语写作：句子·段落·篇章 . 北京：外语教学与研究出版社 .

孙有中，张莲 . 2016. 大学英语思辨教程写作 3：议论文写作 . 北京：外语教学与研究出版社 .

威廉姆 . 2017. 大学学术英语读写教程（上册）. 上海：上海外语教育出版社 .

吴慧坚 . 2019. 英语修辞入门 . 北京：外语教学与研究出版社 .

伍忠杰，余渭深，王海啸 . 2013. 新大学英语综合教程·卓越篇 . 北京：高等教育出版社 .

张在新 . 2010a. 英语写作教程 1. 北京：外语教学与研究出版社 .

张在新 . 2010b. 英语写作教程 2. 北京：外语教学与研究出版社 .

张在新 . 2010c. 英语写作教程 3. 北京：外语教学与研究出版社 .

张在新 . 2010d. 英语写作教程 4. 北京：外语教学与研究出版社 .